the spanish

ABOUT THE BOOK

The forging of the Spanish character — the land of the Cid, the Moors, American gold, the intrepid nation on whose empire the sun never set — the glory that was and is Spain. The castles, the heroes, the invincible armies — these have made Spain the intrepid nation.

From the familiar Spain of today, Lowe travels back with us to the great events, the great men, who have made Spain what she is.

ABOUT THE AUTHOR

Alfonso Lowe first visited Spain 50 years ago when he walked from Bilbao on the Atlantic coast all the way to Barcelona on the Mediterranean earning his meals on the way (partly as an odd-job man in a French circus). Since then he has visited Spain frequently.

Born in Liverpool, he practised medicine in Africa until his retirement in 1970. Since then he and his wife have lived in Catalonia in Spain and he has devoted himself to writing about Mediterranean subjects — Venice, Sicily and Spain. He has published over 200 papers on medical subjects, anthropology, mathematics and heraldry and was elected Correspondent of the Córdoba Royal Academy in 1972. His *Companion Guide To Southern Spain* has earned him the reputation of one of the finest writers on Spain.

Alfonso Lowe

Correspondent of the Córdoba Royal Academy

the spanish

THE INTREPID NATION

GORDON CREMONESI

Ce peuple intrépide, où les femmes combattaient comme les hommes, où il était inouï qu'un mourant poussât un soupir, pouvait être vaincu cent fois, jamais subjugué.

J. Michelet, *Histoire de la République romaine*, 1866

(This intrepid people, whose women fought like men, whose dying men were never heard to gasp, could be defeated a hundred times, subjugated never.)

Designed by Heather Gordon-Cremonesi
Produced by Chris Pye
Set by Preface Ltd, Salisbury
Printed in Great Britain by The Anchor Press Ltd

The publishers wish to thank
The Witch Ball Print Shop, Brighton
for their help in finding illustrations

946 LOWE

100082825

ISBN 0-86033-006-0

Gordon Cremonesi Publishers
New River House
34 Seymour Road
London N8 0BE

Contents

Preface   9
Introduction – the Heart of Spain   13

PART I – PEOPLE
 1   Early Invaders   37
 2   The Coming of Islam   55
 3   Emirs, Caliphs and their Downfall   67
 4   The Road Back   85
 5   The Men from Morocco   95
 6   The Trastámaras   105
 7   Founders of Empire   117
 8   The Golden Century and After   131

PART II – PLACES
 9   The Roman Legacy: Tarragona   149
10   Islamic Survivals   159
11   Traces of the Visigoths   175
12   The Pilgrims' Way: León and Burgos   189
13   The Renaissance in Spain: Salamanca   203

Further Reading   216

Notes   219
Index   223

Santiago
GALICIA
R. Miño
Oviedo
ASTURIA
León
LEÓN
PORTUGAL
Burgos
OLD CASTILE
Segovia
Salamanca
Madrid
Tagus
Toledo
Mérida
NEW CASTILE
R. Guadiana
Córdoba
Guadalquivir
Seville
ANDALUSIA
Granada
Cádiz
Málaga
Almería
Gibraltar
MOROCCO
Pamplona
FRANCE
NAVARRE
Gerona
CATALONIA
Barcelona
R. Ebro
Zaragosa
ARAGON
Tortosa
Tarragona
Teruel
R. Turia
BALEARIC
ISLES
R. Jucar
Valencia
MURCIA
Alicante
Cartagena

Preface

Two hundred years ago E. F. Lantier felt the need to explain why he was launching "yet another book on Spanish travel". Since his day there has been no slackening of the output and travellers, famous or forgotten, have continued to pour out descriptions, illustrations and impressions. To add to the offerings of such authors as Richard Ford, George Borrow, Théophile Gautier, Gustave Doré, Prosper Mérimée and Alexandre Dumas calls for an explanation as much as it did in Lantier's day.

The writers mentioned above rarely succeeded in suppressing their national prejudices; indeed, like others, such as the Duke of Wellington, they made little attempt to do so. "The only way to get them to do anything", he wrote, "is to frighten them, to take a decided line". Hence possibly the lack of co-operation of which he had to complain so often. Nor did Ford, who reported this, conceal his own sense of superiority and in this respect he was very Spanish. For the Spaniard is by no means convinced that he or his way of life are in any way inferior to ours. True, the modern annual influx of tourists persuades many young Spaniards that there must be some virtue in vulgarity and vociferousness, for otherwise why can the foreigner travel for pleasure while the Spaniard goes abroad to make a living?

Perhaps we should give more thought to the Spaniard's temperament, and especially his obstinacy, so often revealed in his dogged courage. Is it linked with his need for liberty, the force that has always made him a democrat? For he is by nature more democratic than we are and it is his very obsession with personal freedom that has always made democratic government in Spain a failure.

When the illiterate Sancho Panza was enthroned as governor of Barataria he asked his steward to read some words printed on the wall. He objected strongly whe he heard himself described as Don Sancho Panza. "Then take notice", he said, "that I'm no Don, and there has never been a Don in my whole family. Plain Sancho Panza's my name . . ." So proud is the Spaniard and so filled with the conviction of his own worth that he has no need to feel offended when not addressed as "Mr Tom", "Mr Dick" or "Mr Harry".

This book tries to present the "feel" of a country through thumbnail biographies of historical figures and brief accounts of some surviving monuments, through *vignettes*, as they used to be called. For, though historians now tend to subordinate the human to the ecological, Spain is essentially the theatre where the former determines the trend of events and the latter merely decides their course. How would we regard a historian of the future who described our century in terms of industry and raw materials only, ignoring the parts played by Hitler, Stalin and Churchill? Hence the importance I attach to the character of the Spaniard, until recently identical with accounts given by the Romans and quite uninfluenced by 300 years under the Visigoths and more than twice that period under Moslem rule.

It will be appreciated that I am out of sympathy with today's emphasis on pragmatism in history to the exclusion of the human element. The trumpet, I feel, is as important as the ticker tape. Spain, though apparently isolated in the farthest corner of Europe, has played a leading and dramatic part in shaping our history. So this book presents some of the colourful characters that can be discerned behind the walls of Toledo and the façades of Salamanca. The reader may decide for himself how far a common bond joins Mariano Alvarez de Castro (Chapter 8) to Viriatus and the defenders of Numantia (Chapter 1). To me the continuity of this intrepid people is plain, revealing a strain that has persisted for over two thousand years, unaltered by Roman perfidy, Visigothic treachery and African duplicity.

The reader may wonder why this book goes no further than the

Peninsular War; he must not think that this arbitrary conclusion was chosen because Spain and the Spaniards have shown any essential change since then. But we may still be too near the events of the last century and the present one to be sure of our judgement. Again, considerations of space preclude embarking on the complicated politics that marked the end of the Spanish Bourbon dynasty and the many examples of brutality and heroism provided by the Carlist Wars. And even if such space had been available it might have been put to better use by following the fortunes of Aragón and Catalonia or by accompanying some of the *conquistadores* in the New World.

This attempt to travel in both time and space may lead the visitor to a greater appreciation of the places he is shown; at least he will avoid such pitfalls as confusing Gothic and Visigothic architecture. For when he sees some of the thousands of survivals of the past in Spain, the traveller is surely entitled to form a mental picture of the kind of people who made them or caused them to be made. And perhaps a rare, enquiring tourist may one day trace the same continuity in the literary arts of Spain and detect Luis de León in Unamuno or Garcilaso de la Vega in Lorca's songs.

Alfonso Lowe
San Pedro de Ribas (Barcelona)

A twisting Toledo street, the Calle de Santa Isabel,

Introduction
~the Heart of Spain

Where shall we look for the traces of "this intrepid people, whose women fought like men . . ."? Somewhere in Spain, far from alien frontiers, there must surely be a city where, in a few hours, we can follow the story of a nation that rose briefly to world power. Madrid is nearest to Spain's geographical centre but Madrid, like most capital cities, reflects its own image and not that of the nation. The centre, perhaps, but not the heart of Spain.

Yet less than an hour's drive away lies Toledo, golden and grim, where you can meet the very essence of Spain, in the stones of her buildings, in the blood of her people. To those who know it, Toledo is indeed the heart of Spain; if Tirso de Molina, creator of Don Juan, made this claim more than three centuries ago, we feel that he was only stating the obvious. In Toledo you can review the legacy of Iberians and Romans, Goths and Arabs, Jews and Castilians, and in her citizens' features recognise their varied ancestry.

Even if you have only one day in Madrid a coach tour will show you something of Toledo. Former travellers made greater sacrifices to see this city of miracles. After his first visit, Alexandre Dumas wrote enthusiastically: "If at any time, Madame, you visit Spain; if you go to Madrid, hire a coach, take a diligence, join a caravan if need be, but go to Toledo, Madame, go to Toledo".

To many, Toledo is the city of El Greco and ornamental cutlery; some may remember the heroism of the siege of the Alcázar. If there were nothing more to be seen I would not advise

13

you to spend a precious day, a week, or even a month, in absorbing its atmosphere. Tourism, catering weak-mindedly for the taste of the average visitor, in a single dose offers him souvenirs and "culture", in the form of El Greco's paintings and a magnificent cathedral. There is much, much more.

Many like to view a city by coach, whisked from one show-piece to another; there are also those who prefer looking at a vase of wild flowers to wandering over a hillside in spring. When Dumas wrote to his mythical "Madame" it was the atmosphere of Toledo that had captured him, not its history, about which he knew little. Those quiet, almost sinister streets that wind round old buildings or through them; the unexpected, crooked *plazas*, each one the source of history or legend; here the Well of Love, round which newly married couples make the circuit that is as important as the wedding ceremony; there the site of the Bitter Well, with its sad story. A town that has been lived in for eight thousand years cannot help exuding some of its essence. See the sights of course, and appreciate them all the more for knowing something of their story, but follow your nose.

Before the Romans came and called it Toletum there was a flourishing Celtiberian town with a foundry. Here were made the swords that the Romans adopted as a standard side-arm for their infantry, and here Toledo steel is still manufactured, as it was in the seventeenth century, when Samuel Butler wrote of "The trenchant blade, Toledo trusty". The secret of its virtue is an open one. The iron comes from the Mondragón mine in the Basque country, already mixed with manganese and ready to absorb carbon. The old pagans, for whom the working of iron had a magical significance, would choose a night when clouds concealed the stars and a warm wind blew from the south; in this obscurity the cherry-red blades could be watched on their way from forge to Tagus and returned for further heating if their colour dimmed before dipping; the virtue of the sand and water of the Tagus did the rest. Of course the chanted invocation to their gods also played its part, altered later to implore the patronage of Christ, the Blessed Virgin and St John.

Roman remains are few and so depleted as hardly to warrant a step aside to look at them. But their stones are still to be found in the walls, which were made up again and again by later masters of the city. The Alcántara Bridge,[1] for instance, has been built and rebuilt by Romans, Visigoths, Moslems and Christians, but many of the stones still show the tell-tale pincer slots used by the Roman engineers to haul them into place.

After the Romans came the Goths, or Visigoths, who made Toledo the capital of their kingdom in 569 A.D. They too built walls, enlarging the area of the city and leaving stretches which can be recognised as their work, as well as at least one surviving gate: the Puerta de Alcántara. It was under the Visigoths that the see of Toledo gained its primacy, still jealously preserved.

But the Visigothic kingdom was riddled with intrigue and at last one faction asked the Moslems of North Africa for help. It took nearly eight centuries of intermittent crusading to get rid of them. Throughout this time we come across descendants of the Visigoths, disguised with Arab names, sometimes allied with the Christians, at others obedient to their Moslem masters. One noble Goth named Fortún kept his lands and authority in this way, and a descendant was Moslem "consul" of Toledo in the ninth century.

Even in legend the downfall of the Visigothic kingom is attributed to depravity and treachery. Julian, governor of Ceuta, is said to have sent his daughter Florinda to the royal court of Toledo as to a "finishing" school. The king, Roderick, watched her bathing in the Tagus and, overcome by her beauty, seduced her; her father's revenge was to invite the Arabs into Spain. From the (possible) site of the royal palace you get a distant view of an old ruin that is called the Bath of Florinda. You will conclude that either the maiden's charms were ample or the king's eyesight phenomenal.

The Arabs and Berbers stayed in Toledo for nearly four centuries and made it a centre of learning. From here ancient knowledge, forgotten in the days of the barbarians, gradually percolated through Western Christianity. Not that the Goths were wholly backward: on the contrary, Toledo had been the seat of the church councils, which I shall mention, and a pathway by which the immense erudition of St Isidore reached a young world eager for culture.

The Moslem occupation was responsible for many legends, of which the invention of marzipan is one. Another concerns the daughter of a Moorish king, Mamun. Her name was Casilda and her

The Bridge of Alcantara overshadowed by the Alcázar and the Convento de la Concepción Francisca.

nature tender; so kind was she that she used to make secret trips to the dungeons, bringing bread to starving Christian prisoners. One day she met her father on her way down and was sternly asked what she was carrying in her apron. In fear she stammered "roses" and, on being commanded to let go the apron, out fell, not the bread she had been carrying, but — roses. In order to be canonised she had of course to be converted and she then became the patron saint of Burgos. She died in 1126 and there is an annual pilgrimage to her tomb, near Briviesca. It is interesting to note that the same miracle is told of St Elizabeth of Hungary, who lived a century later?

If any town had to be chosen for the survival of organised Christianity under the Moslems, it would be Toledo. Not only had it been honoured with the primacy under the Visigoths, but it remained the seat of the Metropolitan, spiritual leader of the Mozarabs, or Christian inhabitants in Islamic territory. In mediaeval times, story-tellers picked on Toledo as typical of Moslem rule and, wanting to compose something really sensational, related how Charlemagne seduced the daughter of the Moslem King Galafre of Toledo. As there never was such a king, and as

Puerta del Sol.

Charlemagne never went further into Spain than the fields round Zaragoza, we must reject the tale, unlike that of St Casilda, who really existed.

But Toledo was not simply the home of love and charity under the Moslems. Its history was, in fact, a long succession of revolts, culminating in virtual independence. After a fruitless siege by the emir of Córdoba, ruler of Islamic Spain, Haqem I sent a strong man of Toledo as governor; he was a *muladí*, which is a converted Christian or the descendant of one. It was a strange choice, for the principal dissidents were also *muladíes*. Amrus, as he was called, had a fortress built where the present Alcázar stands (and where the Romans probably had their fort:[2]). Arab building was typically of stamped earth, as can be seen all over the south of Spain, and the lofty fortress needed so much earth that a huge ditch or borrow-pit was left. The dissidents were next invited to a state banquet, to meet the visiting heir apparent. They were admitted one by one and murdered one by one. Then the bodies — they say seven hundred of them — were thrown into the ditch. The episode is called "The Day of the Ditch" (Arabic: *waq'at al hufra*; Spanish: *la jornada del foso*) and if you have had a bad night, you still call it *una noche toledana*. The result of the lesson was five more revolts in the next twenty years.

In 1085 Toledo fell to the Christians, under Alfonso VI, and was never retaken, even by the fearsome hordes of wild African tribesmen who succeeded the easy-going, pleasure-loving descendants of the original invaders and their Spanish women. The most important feature of the Christian conquest was the capture of a huge library which, under the guidance of Archbishop Raymond and his successors, continued the task of enlightening Western Europe. Thus was born the school of translators which flourished for over two hundred years, until misplaced zeal and bigotry dispersed it.

I mentioned the wild tribesmen who crossed from North Africa; for a time it looked as though the whole of Spain would fall into their hands. They defeated Alfonso VI time and again, but Toledo held firm. During the reign of his grandson came its sternest test. Alfonso VII was besieging Oreja when the main Moorish army surrounded Toledo, defended by the Empress Berenguela. Failing to capture the city by assault, the Moslems began devastating the fields round about. Then a message came from Berenguela: "Thus says the Empress, wife of the Emperor. Do you not see that you are fighting against a woman and that this does you little honour? If you want to fight, go to Oreja and fight with the Emperor, who is waiting for you in battle order." At this the Moslem leaders looked up and beheld her seated on a canopied throne, on the highest tower of the Alcázar, dressed as befits an empress and surrounded by a troop of damsels, singing and accompanying themselves with drums, cithers, cymbals and psalteries. The Moslem leaders were much ashamed to see this; they bowed in salutation and marched their army back home.

The end of the Moorish threat came in 1212, with the battle of Las Navas de Tolosa. It was in Toledo that the allies assembled before marching south to victory; it was in Toledo that they commemorated the mysterious shepherd (perhaps a saint in disguise) who showed them the secret mountain path that led them to victory and it was in Toledo that St Ferdinand, king and conqueror, founded a cathedral to glorify the crowning victory.

Why then, you may ask, is Toledo no longer the capital of Spain? In its area of less than a square mile 200,000 inhabitants formerly lived under the benign rule of Moslems and Christians; its decline into a squalid home for a tenth of that number in the eighteenth century is said to have been caused by the arrogance of the church dignitaries. Philip II, of Armada fame, had brought the royal court from Valladolid to Toledo in 1559 but had his fill of the haughty clergy after a year and moved to Madrid, which thus became the first and last fixed capital of Spain since the defeat of the Visigoths in 711.

Toledo occupies a granite bluff surrounded on the east, south and west by the River Tagus. You approach it after an hour's run from Madrid, across the fertile *vega*, between the bull-ring on your right and the remains of the Roman amphitheatre on your left. (It is strange how, in many Spanish towns, the two are scarcely 100 yards apart, as though tradition had dedicated the spot to the spectacle of bloodshed.) The huge building you see just beyond the bull-ring is the Hospital of St John the Baptist, a good example of Spanish Renaissance architecture dating from 1541. Inside we find El Greco's portrait of the founder, Cardinal Juan de Tavera, and his sumptuous marble tomb, by the younger Berruguete. It contrasts with that of Archbishop Fernández Portocarrero in the Cathedral, which carries the legend, *Hic jacet pulvis cinis et nihil* (here lie dust, ashes and nothing). But here, in the Hospital of St John, the art lover will spend time that he will regret later, admiring paintings by, or attributed to such masters as Coello, Caravaggio, Ribera (a bearded woman suckling an infant), Titian, Tintoretto and, of course, El Greco. You may call me a Philistine but I am not the only one who gets more enjoyment out of the eighteenth-century pharmacy.

If you look east across the Tagus you see the King's Garden – *la huerta del rey* – where Alfonso VI spent a year of exile as the guest of his Moslem vassal, Mamun, the father of St Casilda. The great army assembled there, the first joint enterprise of León, Castile, Aragón and Navarre, on its way to Las Navas de Tolosa. There was a large French contingent too, which left in disgust when restrained from plundering the wealthy Jews of Toledo. The castle that you see to the south is the over-restored San Servando, now a high school.

You enter Toledo round the Visagra Gate – the new one built in 1550; the old one, the only Islamic ninth-century gate still standing, can be seen a little to the west. For those who become interested in the Visigothic horseshoe arch, it is useful to know

General view of Toledo dominated by the Alcázar.

why this one is so confidently ascribed to the Moslems who succeeded them. The answer is that the latter introduced the *alfiz*, or rectangular "label" over doors and windows, that can be seen over the interior gate. This venerable gate is chiefly remembered as the one through which Alfonso entered Toledo on the historic day of its surrender.

Go back to the main road and enter the city. After a short walk, turn round and you will see the patterned roof of coloured tiles that crowns the gate towers of the "new" Visagra Gate and the arms of Charles V over the arch. On your left is the *mudéjar*[3] tower of Santiago del Arrabal, the church of St James of the Suburb. It has a special interest, as it is one of the few genuine relics of a minaret in Toledo, at least up to its bell housing. If you are not in a hurry, go in and admire the lofty proportions of the church and the delicately carved stucco of the pulpit, from which the firebrand St Vincent Ferrer preached. He converted Jews by the hundred, through fear of hell-fire either in the next world, or in this.

Your road then brings you opposite an impressive mediaeval monument, the Puerta del Sol (Gate of the Sun) and, by passing through the adjacent Roman-Visigothic Gate of Valmardón, you may enter the upper gallery. To see a rare antique, walk on a few steps and there, on your left, is a tenth-century mosque, now known as San Cristo de la Luz. It is said that when Alfonso VI entered the city his horse stopped outside the mosque and knelt down. Investigation revealed a crucifix in the thickness of the wall and a Visigothic lamp still burning despite all the centuries which had passed since a Christian church stood there. Inside is an inscription commemorating the miracle and the first mass consequently held there by the Christian conquerors. By an understandable quirk of hero-worship a legend makes the Cid ride at Alfonso's side during the triumphant entry, and it is the Cid's famous charger Babieca that bows his knee. I mention this variant reluctantly, as the Cid was in Zaragoza in May, 1085, when Toledo fell.

As you look round the tiny oratory, note that the columns have Visigothic capitals and that the nine bays have concave ceilings, each with a different pattern of vaulting but all of oriental type. Above the lattice work over the entrance the illustration shows an inscription in Cufic Arabic, constructed of brick and giving the date of its completion, in our reckoning, as 999 A.D. The church is much larger than the original oratory of the Moslems, as a two-storey *mudéjar* annexe was added after the reconquest of the city. Even more remarkable is the Church of El Salvador (if you can find someone to open it), near that of Santo Tomé, where you are *always* taken to see El Greco's masterpiece, "The Burial of Count Orgaz". Renovations have disclosed an old mosque with horseshoe arches, in which Roman and Visigothic columns and capitals have been revealed after being covered with plaster for a thousand years. This is yet another church whose bell tower was a minaret, and the masonry and ornamental frieze suggest that it may be even older.

Not far away is the centre of the city's life, the triangular Plaza de Zocodover. The obviously Arabic name is a corruption of *Suk es-sawab*, not quite correctly rendered as "horse market", for the word means any riding-animal and the correct translation takes us back to a far more picturesque scene. We can hear the whinny of arabs and barbs, the braying of donkeys and the bubbling groan of camels, the rising voices of the hagglers, the cry of the water-sellers and the persistent drone of the beggars; we can recapture the smells of an oriental bazaar under a general pall of dust. The scene is not so different on a summer's evening in our own time: dust has been eliminated and the stink of inferior petrol takes its place, the hagglers have given way to the milling crowds of the *paseo* and the officers and cadets of the military college, punctiliously saluting as they pass and pass again. The beggars are no longer allowed to whine, but they will pluck your sleeve, and the blind sellers of lottery tickets preserve the oriental atmosphere with their long drawn-out cry of "To be drawn today!", *para hoy*, in ascending notes of a minor key.

Above you towers the Alcázar, rebuilt so often that it has no resemblance to the original. For centuries criminals were brought from there to the Zocodover where they were executed and their heads, pickled in brine, nailed up. On the east side is the Arch of the Blood — nothing to do with executions, or at least not directly. It was named after an image, the "Cristo de la Sangre", placed here so that passers-by could utter a prayer. A brotherhood of friars, the *Hermandad de la Sangre*, took its name from the image and attended the condemned in their final hour. Through the arch, down the steps and on your left is the beautiful Hospital de Sante Cruz, a gem of plateresque architecture (the term, explained later, denotes a style of the Spanish Renaissance), now housing the Provincial Museum. Originally built for Cardinal Pedro Mendoza, it still displays the family arms and their motto *Ave Maria gratia plena*, and has patios with double rows of arcades and an *artesonado*[4] ceiling.

But it is in the streets that you are most aware of the flavour of the past. At night, between the brown, stone buildings, under the street lamps on their wrought-iron brackets, it is easy to imagine the hooded familiars of the Inquisition hurrying their victim away from contact with the world, perhaps to see the light of day only once more, on the way to the place of burning. Even by day the alert wanderer cannot but be aware of the continuity of history. Go west from the Plaza de Zocodover and you come upon the *mudéjar* Church of San Vicente. A museum with a wealth of artistic treasures – among them numerous El Grecos, of course – it still conveys an intimate touch, a Roman frieze this time, on the southern aspect of the bell tower.

A little further on, in the Calle Esteban Illán, is the Casa de Mesa. Entering on the first floor of a seedy apartment house, you come upon the most splendid *mudéjar* interior in Toledo. To see the *artesonado* is to enjoy the greatest delight of Arab decoration. We bless inspiration that transformed the whole floor from a private flat into the local Institute of Fine Arts and History, and arrested its slow decay.

On again, and you emerge in a dusty, depressing square, whose last old buildings have been pulled down to make way for low blocks of cleaner but repulsive aspect. This is the Plaza de Padilla, where stood the mansion of one of the leaders of the civic rising of 1520. Though his name lives on his house was pulled down after his execution and a tablet set up forbidding for ever the erection of another building. Juan Padilla is made immortal here; his wife, María Pacheco, was more remarkable. We shall meet her at the Alcázar.

Nearby was the house of a contemporary, who fought for the Emperor Charles V while his brother joined the revolt. He too died young, in the service of his master, instead of on the scaffold; but four kind centuries have blurred the details of right and wrong. It was Garcilaso de la Vega who lived here, the soldier who in his brief life and with his sparse works did what so few have achieved, combining the sensitivity of the poet with the elegance of a supreme craftsman and gaining world renown in his short lifetime.

More mysterious, narrow streets, some only shadowy passages, bring you to the Church of San Juan de los Reyes – St John because Isabel and Ferdinand adopted the Baptist as their patron, and *Reyes* because they were joint sovereigns, neither subject to the other. All round the apse are votive fetters, removed from Christian captives as the war against Granada progressed; the ones you see came from the captives at Ronda.

The church in a way sums up the reign of the Catholic Sovereigns. It was planned in 1476 when Isabel and Ferdinand made their own lands safe against Christian rivals, and was intended to be their sepulchre until the conquest of Granada offered them a more fitting memorial. Its style is a florid, decadent Gothic, best seen in the cloister, that survived in Spain long after the Renaissance took hold elsewhere; its interior decoration is peculiarly Spanish in that Gothic themes and lettering are treated in the manner of oriental surfaces. The artisans who stayed on under new, Christian masters built to Christian plans, but the flavour of the East remains as pervasive as

The Renaissance
doorway of the
Museum of Santa Cruz.

the whiff of garlic in an *olla*.

You are standing on a bluff, from which you may look down on the western stretch of the Tagus, where it is crossed by the beautiful Bridge of San Martín. Like most historic monuments, this one shows traces of a train of incarnations, the last, of 1690, giving it its present character. The illustration also shows San Juan de los Reyes on the hill and the towers of the Puerta del Cambrón on the extreme left.

If you turn north and follow the old town wall you pass the slaughter house, where King Roderick's palace is said to have stood when he watched the fair Florinda bathing. The palace was not there; King Roderick (as I shall explain) was not there; and if Florinda was there she would hardly have been bathing at the tower entrance to a public bridge, which is what her "bath" was.

Soon you come to the gate called Puerta del Cambrón, originally Visigothic or earlier but many times done over, as you can tell from the Roman stones. Down the steep hill outside stands the Church of Santa Leocadia, or rather "stood", for of the old Visigothic building nothing remains except a single, lonely column in the garden and the memory of the Councils of Toledo

The bridge of San Martin and above it San Juan de los Reyes. At the far end of the bridge is the Puerta del Cambrón.

that held their meetings here. It is now a good example of *mudéjar* building and is usually called "San Cristo de la Vega"; its final restoration was in 1826 and it is visited for the wooden crucifixion, in which the Redeemer's right hand hangs stiffly down.

The legend that grew up round the figure was immortalised by Zorrilla in the last century. It concerns a girl, seduced by a soldier after he had sworn before the image to marry her. On his return from the wars, intoxicated with fame, he denied the oath, even before the court to which she brought him. Her only witness was the image of the crucified Christ and in desperation she demanded that her plea be placed before it. It was done and, as she knelt and asked, "Lord, do you not remember this man's promise to marry me?", a more than mortal voice replied, "I swear it", and a wooden hand detached itself from the cross and touched the record of witnesses. A banal and sentimental tale, but it gains stature in Zorrilla's verse. The more mundane explanation of the abnormal crucifixion is that it formed the central figure in a group portraying the Deposition from the Cross, and that the others were lost. Such groups are still to be seen in many parts of Spain.

But you will be in a hurry, if you hope to get at least an impression of Toledo's many faces in a day. You will therefore turn south from San Juan de los Reyes and, instead of visiting San Cristo de la Vega, walk through the old Jewish quarter. Here was said to have been enacted the story of the fair Rachel, with whom Alfonso VIII was so infatuated that he left his bride, Eleanor of Lancaster, and disappeared into a house in the ghetto for seven years. How the nobles of Castile solved the problem was told by the sixteenth-century dramatist Lope de Vega, eventually reaching German audiences through Grillparzer's tragedy *Die Jüdin von Toledo*. On your left is the church of Santa María la Blanca, formerly a part-time synagogue where each of the three faiths could hold its service on the appropriate day – Friday, Saturday and Sunday. It was built some time after the reconquest, a monument to Christian tolerance; its seizure and conversion into a church in 1405, at the instigation of St Vincent Ferrer, is a reminder of bigotry. It is safe now as a national monument and every year thousands of visitors admire its octagonal columns, its horseshoe arches and its *mudéjar* decoration. They are rarely told that some of the earth beneath their feet was brought from Mount

Zion by an intrepid Jewish mediaeval traveller.

The other synagogue reminds us of the days of Pedro the Cruel, who prevailed on the Black Prince to invade Spain and restore him to his throne. Pedro's treasurer, Samuel Leví, wielded great influence; his mansion occupied the site of the later house of El Greco and hard by is the synagogue he built, now named "El Tránsito" from its later dedication to the Death of the Virgin. The work was done by *mudéjares* and the ornamental stucco surfaces are among the best of their kind. You have already seen San Juan de los Reyes and the Museum of Santa Cruz and will now understand where the intricate "plateresque" style of low relief had its inspiration.

Among the numerous Hebrew inscriptions is one of praise to the Lord, to Samuel Leví and to "King Don Pedro; and may God be his help and enlarge his estates and prosper him and exalt him and set his seat above all princes". Alas for the efficacy of prayer! Pedro certainly strove for prosperity by arresting Leví, charging him with appropriating royal revenue, and killing him after eliciting under torture the whereabouts of his treasure. But he did not long survive him. The complicated cellars under the gardens of El Greco's house are said to have been the hiding place of the treasure. Once they may also have concealed the fabulous Girdle of Zobeida, so closely linked with Spain's history.

The House of El Greco was occupied by the artist for part of the year 1585 and it was the Marqués de la Vega-Inclán who generously donated the house and adjacent museum, furnished at his own expense in authentic sixteenth-century style. One of its greatest charms is that it typifies the Toledan suburban villa, the *cigarral*, where foliage, shade and gurgling springs welcome the owner on the evening of a hot summer's day. They are typically Spanish, unlike El Greco.

The recent vogue for the great Cretan painter is due largely to two artists, Utrillo and Santiago Rusiñol. It was the latter – painter, eccentric, morphinist – who astounded Madrid at the beginning of this century by his enthusiasm for the unknown Greek who had made his home in Toledo. Before long it had reached its climax in the city of El Greco's adoption. Like the ornamental, damascened cutlery that I mentioned earlier, largely imported for sale to the tourist, there is nothing Toledan and little Spanish about El Greco. A Cretan brought up in the Byzantine tradition, he came to Spain primed with Tintoretto's Venetian mannerism. He learned nothing from Spanish artists; they acquired nothing from him. Study him, enjoy him, read about him, but don't think of his art as Spanish. And remember that Toledo would still be the marvel that it is, had El Greco never lived there. What is usually called his finest painting, *The Burial of Count Orgaz*, is, as I mentioned earlier, the showpiece of the nearby Church of Santo Tomé, of which he was a benefactor. If you have not been sated by the works you have just seen, you will enjoy the change from somewhat monotonous saints to the portraits of notables standing round the grave. Don't, by the way, forget to look at the bell tower, another converted minaret.

An interesting story tells how Santo Tomé ceased to be a mosque, though authorised to continue as such when Toledo was captured by Alfonso VI. The Empress Berenguela was caught in a storm one day and sought shelter in the mosque which, at the time, belonged to the strict Malekí sect. Though no gentile was allowed to enter an exception was made in this case. She seems to have had the knack of inspiring chivalry in Moslem breasts, but chivalry is no substitute for piety; the precincts had been desecrated and nothing could make them clean again. They were therefore handed over to the Christians.

The massive Cathedral is worthy of the many books that have been written about it. A treasure house of Spanish history and an art gallery combined, no passing mention of mine could do it justice. Such richness (*Dives Toletana* it was called) deserves more, but I shall nevertheless venture a few rambling remarks. You must certainly see the woodcarvings of the conquest of Granada, executed by Rodrigo Alemán within three years of the event. Get one of the *azotaperros* – the uniformed watchmen are still called "dog beaters" or "whippers-out" – to open the wrought-iron gates of the *coro* (Toledo still has its choir in the traditional site, the centre of the nave) and bring your own torch.

Afterwards, standing before the high altar, you will see that one of the statues facing you on the right is dressed as a Moslem, surely a surprising figure to find among the saints. When Alfonso VI captured Toledo in 1085 one of the articles of surrender was his undertaking that the Moslems should be allowed to retain their religion and their chief mosque, which had replaced a Visigothic church and stood on the site of the present Cathedral. A year later, while he was away, the Queen and Archbishop Berbard took forcible possession of the mosque; Alfonso returned in time and was so enraged at having his royal word broken that he ordered the archbishop to be burned, the Queen presumably not being expendable. Here you may see the different attitudes shown towards the Moslems by a Spaniard of that time and by a French queen and prelate. At this juncture the saintly Abu Walid, whose statue you see, saved the archbishop by surrendering the mosque.

In the site now directly opposite stands the legendary shepherd of Las Navas de Tolosa, who guided the Christian armies through the mountains and enabled them to win the overwhelming victory of 1212 against the fanatical Moors of North Africa.

If we are to note in the Cathedral only those features that are peculiar to Toledo, I must confess that these are few. The building, for all its proportions and beauty, could just as well be anywhere else in Spain or France. The Chapel of the Constable, a riot of florid Gothic, is almost duplicated in Burgos and possibly again in Murcia. The mozarabic chapel, however, is almost unique, for it and the Old Cathedral of Salamanca are the only consecrated sites where the mozarabic rite – the liturgy of the Visigoths – is regularly celebrated.

One day, when you are going back to the Cathedral, spend a little time on its surroundings. The Town Hall (*Ayuntamiento*) opposite the south-western angle shows you the typical "Herrera" façade of the late Spanish Renaissance, built by the son of El Greco. Facing the east end is a narrow street leading to the headquarters and prison of the Holy Brotherhood, whose fifteenth-century doorway is surmounted by the arms and devices of the Catholic Sovereigns. The *Santa Hermandad* arose in the twelfth century, along with Castile's pioneer parliamentary experiment, as a confederation of cities bound by agreement to the defence of their civil liberties. When Isabel came to the throne the most pressing need was the restoration of public order in town and country; overcoming much opposition, especially from the noble bandits who had brought Castile to the verge of ruin, she transformed the institution from a private league to the New Brotherhood, a national police force paid for by the cities. It was empowered to administer summary justice and the death sentence was executed by making the condemned a target for crossbow practice. If you look at the royal escutcheon again you will see

(left) The Crucifixion within San Cristo de la Vega.

(below) Interior of the Synagogue.

(opposite above) San Cristo de la Luz.

(opposite below) The façade of San Juan de los Reyes.

that the supporters are archers. They are the distant ancestors of today's *Guardia civil* whose members may be seen in pairs on foot, on horseback, on motor-cycles or as a road patrol and first-aid squad, in any part of Spain. Though the Hermandad served its purpose its members became as unpopular as the highwaymen they brought to justice. Don Quixote is roughly handled by a troop leader in the adventure of Maritornes and the muleteer, and after the liberation of the galley slaves it is hard to know whether the criminals or Sancho Panza are more terrified of the dreaded Brotherhood.

By now you will surely feel that you have seen two millennia of history. Only one more visit is required of you, to the Alcázar, the noble fortress palace that crowns the highest ground of Toledo. It is possibly the successor of Iberian and Roman citadels, and certainly of the Islamic fortress; on its roof sat the Empress Berenguela and her damsels, shaming the infidels. The building you see is (so far) the last of a long series of reconstructions. You are told that it is an exact reproduction of the Renaissance building put up for the Emperor Charles V, who is said to have remarked that he really felt like an emperor when he descended the grand staircase. However, it is unlikely that he spent any time there and the present building bears little resemblance to that of a contemporary drawing. His son Philip II began the change and since then it has had many misadventures. The combined British, German and Portuguese troops burned it down when they had to retire in 1710, during the War of the Spanish Succession. The French did the same in 1810 and a careless Spanish cadet set the third reconstruction on fire in 1887.

The basement stables have been the pride of the Alcázar since the sixteenth century and it was here that the nationalists held out in 1936, while the rest of the fortress was methodically blasted away by the besiegers' guns, planes and land mines. They show the telephone over which the commander, Colonel Moscardó, was instructed to hand over the Alcázar if he wished to see his son alive again. With a refinement of cruelty the besiegers allowed father and son to converse over the same instrument. Both showed the obstinate heroism that has always characterised the Spaniard; you will read how the governor of Tarifa reacted to the same threat over six centuries earlier (Chapter 1).

Michelet[7], in his history of the Romans, stated that among

The headquarters of the
Santa Hermandad.

the Spaniards the women too were warriors. It is of course not an
exclusively Spanish attribute and most nations can cite females,
such as Joan of Arc, who were distinguished warriors. Of the
Spanish, one of the bravest soldiers at the bloody battle of
Lepanto turned out to be a woman and they maintained their
record in the Civil War of 1936–9. None, however, achieved the
fame of María Pacheco, widow of the Juan de Padilla whom we
met earlier. This young woman, in whose veins flowed the blood
of the haughty Pachecos and Mendozas, would not accept the
defeat of the *Comuneros* (see Chapter 8) and the loss of her
husband. Typifying the nation that "could be defeated a hundred
times, subjugated never", she roused the citizens of Toledo, who
carried her in triumph to the Alcázar, and then went out to fight
the Emperor's troops. From the roof she looked across the river
and watched the fighting round the castle of San Servando; she
saw the enemy entrenched on every side; she saw the summer pass
and bitter winter add to the miseries of the besieged. At last, ten
months after the cause of the *Comuneros* was lost, she capitulated.
But the loyalists, who had put a price on her head, were not to
have the satisfaction of capturing this indomitable woman.

Dressed as a labourer's wife, mounted on a donkey and carrying a brace of ducks, as though to market, she rode boldly through the besiegers and made her way to Portugal. There she died ten years later, aged forty, unforgiving and unforgiven.

Alvonso VII ("The Emperor") in the Cathedral at Santiago.

PART I
people

The statue of Viriatus at Zamora.

CHAPTER ONE

Early Invaders

Our first accounts of Spain list over thirty different tribes, many of them speaking languages unintelligible to the rest. Called Iberians, they are thought to have come from North Africa and to have followed their northward course to France and Britain through Spain. Perhaps the Basques of the western Pyrenees are their only pure descendants. Ages later masses of Celts passed through the Pyrenees and settled in the plains, mixing with the Iberians in the heart of the country, producing a new national unit, the Celtiberians.

We know something about the Celts, an early wave in the series of spreading Indo-European ripples. They were well known to the Romans, having frequently invaded central Italy; they besieged and, though the Romans disliked admitting it, captured Rome itself and sold it back to the Romans. Sections of this warrior people settled, not only in Spain, but also in the British Isles, the Gaul which is now France and the Cisalpine Gaul of northern Italy. One contingent travelled down the Danube and sacked the treasuries of Delphi in the third century B.C., while another crossed into Asia Minor and settled down as the Galatians. Wherever they went they left names containing the syllable *Gal* (or its equivalent *Wal*). Thus Strabo, in the first century B.C., refers to the "Celts or Galaticos" and hence also Wales, Galway, Donegal, Portugal, Galicia in Spain and south-eastern Europe, Wallachia of Rumania, the Walloons of Belgium and the Valais of Switzerland. Wherever they went they showed a ferocious bravery and a preference for death rather than slavery. In the Museo Nazionale in Rome is the famous statue of a Gaul about to take his own life after a defeat, having already killed his wife. Perhaps there is a special significance in Paul's message to the Galatians (4:31): "So then, brethren, we are not children of the bondwoman, but of the free. Stand therefore in the liberty wherewith Christ has made us free, and be not entangled again with the yoke of bondage."

The Iberians were subdued far less easily than even the Celts. Whereas Caesar brought the Gauls to obedience in ten years, the Spaniards held out for two hundred. The Celtiberians were toughest of all; though they were shepherds and cultivators, fighting was their chief occupation and fighting each other filled in the time between resisting foreign invaders. Between fights, says Strabo, they showed a contemptuous negligence – *oligoria*; normally their days were occupied in fighting or sleeping, while their women ploughed the fields and reaped the harvests. Much later, during the Peninsular War, the same alternating indolence and tenacity aroused exasperation and respect in the breasts of the Spaniard's British allies.

Our first record of their superhuman endurance goes back to two centuries before Christ. Carthage had been soundly beaten by Rome in the first Punic War; to retrieve her losses in Sicily she reverted to expansion in Spain, whose warriors made excellent mercenaries. But they also made formidable opponents. Hamilcar Barca's death at Elche, fighting the wild, disorganised Iberians, was a prelude to the difficulties that all invaders have met. By 220 B.C. Hamilcar's son Hannibal had been as far as Salamanca, fighting and recruiting; then he met resistance at the east coast Iberian town of Saguntum, which had a treaty of alliance with Rome. Refusing to surrender, the men and women of Saguntum showed more heroism than the Roman allies who left them in the lurch. It took eight months for the flower of the Carthaginian army to conquer them; eight months during which each foot of ground was bought with Carthaginian blood. When the defenders saw that all hope had vanished, they set fire to what remained of the city and perished in the flames rather than be captured.

That was the pattern of Spanish resistance. "This intrepid people" wrote Michelet, "whose women fought like men, whose dying men were never heard to gasp, could be defeated a hundred times, subjugated never. After a battle they sent this message to the victorious Romans, 'We shall allow you to leave Spain, on condition that you give us a suit of clothes, a horse and a sword for each man.' One should not think of taking them prisoner. The Spaniards made the worst slaves. They would kill each other or their masters or, if they were put aboard ship, they would bore through the hull and sink her. They usually carried poison with them so as not to survive defeat."

Seldom did they act in concert with their neighbours, but never did they condescend to surrender: stubborn resistance, starvation, cannibalism, fire and mass suicide was the usual sequence. It was enacted again and again as the result of Rome's superb strategy. For while Hannibal remained invincible in Italy, Rome sent an expeditionary force to Spain. In 209 B.C. the younger Scipio captured Cartagena with an exemplary display of energy and followed this success with a more important exhibition of

The Roman bridge at Mérida.

clemency. But all in vain. By 206 Spain was free of Carthaginians, ready to supply silver, copper, wheat, horses and wine — or so the Romans mistakenly thought.

The Celtiberians of the central plateau and the Lusitanians, inhabiting what is now much of Portugal and western Spain, were the core of the resistance and, says Atkinson, "by 179, when these tribes had too to all appearances been subjected, over 150,000 troops had been drafted to the conquest of this *horrida et bellicosa provincia*, whose fighting spirit had imposed on Rome the necessity for permanent military service".[1] But twenty-five years later the greatest threat of all arose; in Lusitania a shepherd named Viriatus became leader of both tribes by sheer merit and inflicted so many defeats on the Romans that they had to sue for peace. Twice indeed were terms granted and twice repudiated by Rome, so that every form of infamy had to be employed to stamp out the rebellion. In Zamora stands a bronze statue of Viriatus, on a plinth in which is moulded the bronze head of a battering ram, possibly a play on the hero's pastoral origin. The inscription is simple — TERROR ROMANORUM; no further designation is needed for the man whose very name inspired fear in the Roman soldiery. Again and again he defeated them in battle, never descending to their level of barbarity. Happily ignorant of the arts of treachery, or scorning their use, he set only his superb leadership and tactical skill against their bad faith. For fifteen years he defied them; then they succeeded in bribing an assassin to kill him. At last the soiled eagles were masters.

But not for long. If Viriatus tested Rome's power in Central Spain, Numantia almost broke it. With 8,000 inhabitants it held out against the Romans and their allies for nineteen years. General succeeded general, each sustaining a worse defeat. Little sympathy was wasted on them by the Romans; Mancinus, for instance, was handed over naked to the Numantians who, barbarians that they were, had no idea of the proper treatment of prisoners; instead of crucifying him or flaying him alive they sent him back to his compatriots.

Eventually the Roman senate, waiving the letter of their own law in the face of this emergency, chose Scipio Aemilianus, conqueror of Carthage, to end this interminable disgrace. Realising that starvation was the only weapon he could trust, Scipio built six encampments and surrounded the town with his 60,000 troops in a continuous earthwork; during the ensuing year only five youths out of the remaining 4,000 inhabitants succeeded in breaking out, and they were sent back without their hands.

In Numantia, as day followed day, famine succeeded hunger; first leather and then the dead were eaten, and eventually the strong began to kill the weak for food. A deputation came to Scipio, heard his terms and then pointed out that what they had come to request was a day's truce to enable them to arrange their suicide. And three days later a handful of diseased, tottering skeletons was all that Rome could show for twenty years of endeavour, trickery and frustration.

I like to stroll round the wind-swept summit of Numantia (near modern Soria), looking at uncovered traces of the Roman town which succeeded the Celtiberian and to talk to the old couple who guard it. At my first visit they pointed out the site of Scipio's camps, one of them still called Castillejo. "Down there", said the old man, "is the Moorish bridge which you crossed to reach the village of Garray and begin your ascent".

The place is a lonely one and I asked about visitors.

"Indeed yes. In summer we have the Pullmans arriving two and three at a time". I was eager to discover who would be interested. Germans of course, I was told, but the majority of visitors were Spaniards. Yes, this was a pilgrimage; it was of Numantia that Cervantes wrote in the play that 2,000 years later inspires the citizens of Zaragoza to hold out against Napoleon. "See here", went on the custodian, pointing to one of the small monuments which relieve the bareness in front of his house. The inscription it bears is somewhat weathered, for the stone was put up in 1886. It was dedicated to the heroic defenders of Numantia by the regiment of Saint Marcial, then stationed at Burgos, but previously at nearby Soria. Later in Soria, I saw a poster on the wall of a tavern where I was taking a glass of wine; it announced a forthcoming football match between a visiting team from Logroñõ and the locals, who were called – can you guess? – the Club Deportivo de Numancia.

If you visit Sagunto, therefore, you will not be surprised to read, on a marble plaque in the Roman theatre, that a performance of Cervantes' *Numancia* was given here when excavations were completed. For Saguntum and Numantia are the best known of many heroic defences by the early inhabitants. The average Spaniard identifies himself with the Celtiberian, not with the

Roman, who stayed for 600 years, nor the Visigoth, nor, of course, the Moor. Whatever infusions may have diluted his blood he is still the descendant of Viriatus and the men of Numantia.

His history provides a hundred examples of the same heroic obstinacy and a thousand of his inability to act in concert with his fellow Spaniards. In A.D. 1294, when Alonso Pérez de Guzmán was besieged in Tarifa by the Moors, the King of Castile's renegade brother brought Guzmán's son to the wall and threatened to kill him if the town was not surrendered. Guzmán's reply was to toss him a dagger and turn away for "he preferred honour without a son to a son with dishonour". When an uproar announced that the renegade had kept his word Guzmán rushed to the battlements, but on seeing his son's body, he returned to his wife observing that it had been a false alarm, as he had thought the noise was occasioned by an assault. Colonel Moscardó of Toledo, you remember, showed the same constancy in 1936. Even in this the women of Spain are not to be outdone. Feijóo[2] tells of the chatelaine faced with the same choice, who pointed to her organs of generation and told the besiegers that "there she had wherewith to make other sons if they killed that one".

Numantia fell in 133 B.C. but the last strongholds in the north held out until Augustus himself reduced them in 19 B.C. He was a member of the triumvirate, a committee of three who ruled Rome after the killing of Julius Caesar. Several words have passed through Spain to be adopted in other languages but surely "era" had one of the strangest transitions. It started as *aera*, the plural of a Latin word that successively meant metal, bronze and (just as "tin" was used in English slang for over a century and "brass" is now) money. In 38 B.C. Augustus introduced a tax in coin and the event was important enough for the Spaniards to reckon dates from the year of the *aera*. Always conservative, the Spaniards reckoned their era from 38 B.C. until the thirteenth century, while the supposed date of Christ's birth was adopted elsewhere in the fourth century. So when you read mediaeval dates in Spain, be careful to subtract 38 if they are given with the word "era", or even "E", as for instance on all Visigothic tombstones.

Of the distinguished Romans whose visits to Spain have been recorded, the majority, at least until the beginning of our era, came to fight wars. Their most immediate profit from this activity was the adoption of the Spanish short sword; this became standard equipment in the legions and contributed in no small measure to their triumphs. The fighting was at first unavoidable, for the Carthaginians had to be attacked here, at their weakest point, and later the Celtiberians had to be tamed to allow the Romans an opportunity of introducing the material benefits which enriched the western world. And lastly came the Civil War, a kind of free-for-all, from which Julius Caesar eventually emerged victorious, only to be murdered in Rome on the fateful Ides of March in 44 B.C. The belief that Caesar and Pompey fought each other in Spain is a fallacy; Pompey certainly left his name there for posterity, in the city of Pompaelo, now Pamplona, but it was his sons whom Caesar defeated, three years after their father had succumbed to the assassin's dagger.

The Romans were thorough in everything, including pacification. Augustus appeared in Tarragona in the baggy trousers of the natives, hoping in this way to please them, much as George IV did when he wore the kilt in Edinburgh. Once the country was quiet and the last troublesome tribes moved from the Cantabrian mountains to the plains, material benefits could be provided. First came communications, a military as well as a civilian requirement, and 12,000 miles of roads soon criss-crossed the peninsula, among them twenty-nine which ranked as first class. Some of these survive in more modern guise, such as the stretch from Port Vendres (Portus Veneris) to Valencia (Valentia Edetanorum) and that from Zaragoza (Caesarea Augusta) to Lérida (Ilerda).

Where there are roads there must be bridges and in building these the Romans were pre-eminent, as befits a nation whose high priest was called Pontifex Maximus, or Senior Bridge Builder. This must originally have been regarded as a skill verging on the supernatural and strangely enough the popes inherited the title and handed it on to their bishops. Spain provides the world's largest and highest Roman arches in the bridge of Alcántara over the Tagus near the Portuguese frontier, and the longest bridge, with 64 arches over the Guadiana at Mérida.

Another inevitable companion of the Roman road were the cemeteries. They were commonly sited along highways and tell us more about the Hispano-Romans than does any surviving text. There is something extraordinarily poignant in the epitaph of a child "who lived three years, seven months, fourteen days and eight hours". A constant ending is the formula "S.T.T.L. – *sit tibi terra levis* – "may the earth rest lightly on you' ". Here is one from Mérida.

> "Julia Anula, daughter of Caius, lies here. Threatened by unspeakable Hades, she lived a short time. Death carried her off when she counted but eighteen Aprils of her youth. Say to her, traveller, 'May the earth rest lightly on you'. Audila, freedwoman of Caius, twenty-four years old, may the earth rest lightly on you and once more, may the earth rest lightly on you".

Another tombstone, erected by an innkeeper to his "dearest wife", shows a bas-relief of the departed drawing a jug of wine from a cask on trestles.

I mentioned Hispano-Romans purposely. For in Spain the intermarriage of Roman and Iberian stock produced a race with talent equalled nowhere in the Latin world. Included among the writers were the two Senecas and their relative Lucan, as well as Martial and Quintilian.

Martial was a gifted and witty poet, a native of Calatayud. In his racy verses he mentions that the Celtiberians used their own urine as a dentifrice. Strangely enough, I have seen a news item to the effect that the same method is still used in the village of Mensalbas (which was Celtiberian country) to cure toothache. In A.D. 325 Bishop Hosius of Córdoba was so respected that the Emperor Constantine appointed him chairman of the Council of Nicaea, where the unity of the Catholic Church was born. The younger and more famous Seneca, who was also born in Córdoba and spent his youth in Rome, eventually became tutor and counsellor to the Emperor Nero. He is universally regarded as one of the most gifted and original writers of his time; the warm-hearted man keeps peeping through the fence of Stoic philosophy and his moral stature – or at least that of his writings – was such that even the early Christian fathers tried to adopt him posthumously. Tertullian called him "ours" and Augustine exclaimed, "What more could a Christian say than this pagan has said?" Eventually Christian tradition represented him as a friend of the Apostle Paul and even invented a correspondence between them.

How many connect this curious invention with a far wilder coincidence? Seneca's brother Gallio was Roman governor of

Seneca.

southern Greece; when the Jews brought Paul before him Gallio
showed the commen sense of his family. "But if it be a question of
words and names," he told them, "and of your law, look ye to it;
for I will be no judge of such matters" (Acts 18:15). Seneca's
influence for good affected at least three Roman emperors; he
disapproved of gladiatoral combats to the death and his pupil Nero
forbade them, but his gay wit and irreverence for imperial divinity
made him unpopular in certain quarters, as did his knack of
becoming a millionaire while preaching stoicism. At least he
practised his philosophy when the supreme test came: ordered by
his pupil, friend and emperor to take his life, he died like a true
stoic. As Durant said, "Next to Cicero he was the most lovable
hypocrite in history".[3]

Spanish blood also produced four of Rome's best emperors.
Under Trajan the empire attained its greatest size and under
Hadrian its strongest frontiers, one of which still crosses Britain
from the Tyne to the Solway Firth. Marcus Aurelius is known to
most of us as the gentle philosopher; the visitor to Rome can see
his equestrian statue in Michelangelo's Campidoglio and pictorial
histories of his wars on the great column in the Piazza Colonna
and on the Arch of Constantine. Theodosius the Great saved the
eastern half of the Roman empire, shortly to become *the* Roman
Empire, from the conquering Goths whom fate eventually brought
to Theodosius' own country, Spain. His true importance, however,
dates from the first time the Church asserted its ascendancy over

an emperor. It was Archbishop Ambrose of Milan who reproached Theodosius for the massacre of 8,000 citizens of Thessalonika and forbade him access to the altar. When the emperor repented and went to pray as usual in the cathedral at Milan, Ambrose prevented him from entering and ordered him to do penance for his crime. The vigorous discipline prescribed by the Church had to be somewhat softened; but, in Gibbon's words, "It was sufficient that the Emperor of the Romans, stripped of the ensigns of royalty, should appear in a mournful and suppliant posture; and that, in the midst of the church of Milan, he should humbly solicit, with sighs and tears, the pardon of his sins".[4] Of the four Spanish emperors I fancy that Theodosius played the greatest part in shaping the destiny of Europe.

Barbarian incursions into Spain date back to a century before Christ, when a Teutonic tribe called the Cimbri staged a full-scale raid. But the first invasion and occupation took place five centuries later when three tribes, the Alans, the Suevi and the Vandals, were allowed into Gaul as a civil war expedient. The result was their irruption into Spain and the beginning of the end of Roman civilisation there. The Alans and the Vandals leave the stage after only forty years, the Suevi linger on in their small kingdom at the north-west corner of Spain for a century and a half. All they brought to Spain was misery, all they left was an evil memory, a name and a ruined wall. The name is Andalucía, derived from "Vandal", the wall is in Galicia, a few miles from Ponferrada, near the village of Pieros.

The ascent is steep and unrewarding, through the soft earth of vineyards. The hilltop, about one and a half miles in cir-

Roman bas-rieliev from the Mérida museum.

cumference, is surrounded with a rude rampart of slate and flat stones, overgrown with brambles. Wind and rain have flattened the surface and brought the inside up level with the top of the rampart. Here a single family cultivates the whole area formerly occupied by the Suevic town, and their plough still turns up the roof slates, potsherds and bones of their predecessors among the vines and wheat.

The arrival of the Goths in 414 was an event of far greater importance, hailed with relief by the victimised Hispano-Romans. The wanderings of this Teutonic people make a fascinating story but are irrelevant here. We have always been told that the names Visigoth and Ostrogoth signified respectively the western and eastern divisions of the Goths; but it is now known that this race, free from false modesty, called its branches *wesu* (good) and *austra* (resplendent). The Visigoths settled for a time near Constantinople, where they were in constant contact with the Byzantine heirs of Greek and Roman civilisation. They accepted Christianity, the Bible was translated into the Gothic language and they attained the status of allies and guardians of the northern frontier. But alliances were no more binding then than they are now. Soon the Visigoths revolted, defeated and killed a Roman emperor, pillaged their way through Greece and approached Italy along the Adriatic coast. Under the leadership of Alaric they sacked Rome and traversed Italy, but turned back from the straits of Messina after an unsuccessful attempt on Sicily. Shortly afterwards Alaric died at Cosenza and was buried with barbaric splendour and ruthlessness beneath the waters of the Busento. (The fatigue party detailed for the burial were killed, so that no one should survive to point out the site of the grave and its jewels.) His successor Adolphus gives us an indication of the potential greatness of the Visigoths.

Previous barbarian invaders had not passed through the province of which Tarragona was then the capital. It was in A.D. 414 that Adolphus led his Visigoths over the Pyrenees and made Barcelona, still under its old name of Amena, his capital. He had given up the Visigoths' ambition of supplanting the Roman empire and realised that a greater future awaited them as *foederati*, or allies of Rome.

It is possible that his remarkable wife, Galla Placidia, who had been taken from Rome as a hostage and travelled as a prisoner as far as Narbonne, had something to do with his decision. A love match appears to have developed between the Gothic king and this beautiful daughter of one Roman emperor and sister of another. She received a truly magnificent wedding present which was possibly why such settlements were soon restricted, on the grounds of economy, by Visigothic law. Other Germanic tribes placed fewer restrictions on the *morgingcap*, the reward for virginity bestowed immediately after the wedding night. With his usual cynicism Gibbon adds that some cautious maidens were wise enough to stipulate beforehand a present which they were only too sure of not deserving. Galla accompanied her husband in the occupation of part of Spain, survived his assassination at Barcelona and later married the Emperor Constantius III. For years she acted as regent of the Western Roman Empire and, after a life which makes a modern adventure story sound tame, was buried in the mosaic tomb at Ravenna, one of the most glorious productions of Christian art. Her life and adventures underline the ever-decreasing distinction between Roman and barbarian.

Before the Visigoths made their home in Spain several other experiences awaited them. They were given a part of Gaul — the south-western corner — as their country and they held this as *foederati* or allies; at Carcassonne you can see the best surviving example of their type of fortification. In A.D. 451, still as allies of Rome, they formed the backbone of the army which met Attila the Hun, the Scourge of God, at Châlons-sur-Marne and called a halt to his triumphant progress. Shortly afterwards the Huns retired to the borders of Asia.

It had taken 700 years to arrest a flood which had begun by recoiling from the Great Wall of China. The Visigoths were now in a position to bargain with Rome and as a condition of their alliance obtained permission to take the peninsula from the other barbarian tribes who had arrived before them. As well for them that they did so, for another Germanic nation, the Franks, soon defeated the Visigoths in France, forcing them to make their home south of the Pyrenees.

It was not long before the Visigoths dropped the pretence of being Roman allies and declared their own sovereignty; but this did not diminish their respect for Roman civilisation nor their continued desire to learn from the Hispano-Roman population. Their eagerness to do so can be judged from the fact that, within two generations, they abandoned their own language in favour of the current Latin idiom. Recent archaeological finds suggest that the majority of the Goths settled as small farmers alongside the Spaniards, from whom they took two-thirds of their property under the name *sortes Gothicae*. It can still be recognised in place names such as Suertes and Sort; Tierzo, Terça; other similar names commemorate the third which the Spaniards were allowed to keep. The fertile strip south of the Cantabrian mountains received most settlers and was thenceforward called *Campi Gothici*, nowadays "tierra del campo". In this area Gothic settlements, such as Villa Gothorum, can still be recognised in the names Villatoro, Toro and the like. The settlers were continually reinforced by groups of Visigothic refugees drifting in from France through the Pass of Roncesvalles and this working class became culturally assimilated in a short time.

The minority, the ruling caste, spread more widely and secured the peninsula by military domination; they numbered no more than 1,500 families who became the great landowners. Remaining aloof while the humbler settlers in the north were absorbed, they persisted in their aspiration to be regarded as the heirs of Rome. It was this aristocracy – the decadent ruling caste – that provided an image, fortunately false, which later Spanish rulers tried to keep alive. In place of Roman efficiency they introduced the doctrine of racial superiority and, while they made no radical change in Spain or in the Spaniards, set a terrifying example of crime and treachery. So frequently did they assassinate their kings that their average reign was among the shortest recorded;[5] during their frequent civil commotions foreigners were four times summoned to help one or other side. The Byzantines occupied the south of Spain for over fifty years after being called in by Athanagild, and the Franks twice obtained a foothold in the north by coming to help the Gothic kings Witrich and Sisenard in turn. You may ask why there was so little Spanish resistance of the kind I have described. The answer is that the Visigoths were welcomed as liberators from the hardships of the financial collapse of Rome and from the fearful depredations of the earlier waves of barbarians. Such nuclei as did offer resistance were too isolated and too unskilled in the arts of war to hold out for long.

On the credit side, although they showed no inclination to become Spaniards – in fact they called Spain "the nation of the Goths" – the ruling families of the Visigoths tried to adopt

Roman civilisation. Their religious conversion was slower; they were heretic Arians[6] when they became lords of the peninsula and it took more than a hundred years for the Catholic faith to triumph. Perhaps the greatest benefit derived from the continuation of the Ecclesiastical Councils of Toledo, the first having sat in A.D. 400. In these, matters of state policy were discussed and even if some short-sighted measures were recommended, at least the king had the advice of his best educated subjects.

Among the characters that appear during the three centuries of Visigothic rule, St Isidore of Seville stands out. His literary output was prodigious, the *Etymologies*, an encyclopaedia of divine and mundane matters, being one of the brighter lights in the so-called Dark Ages. Copies were eagerly sought by the nations of Western Europe and Isidore remained the final authority in most fields of learning for eight centuries. As Bishop of Seville for forty years, his influence in Spain was great and, on the whole, beneficial.

Isidore's eloquence was remarkable, even among prelates who thought nothing of holding forth for a whole morning. It was believed to have been foretold by a swarm of bees issuing from his mouth while he was still in his cradle. This same story was told two centuries earlier of St Ambrose of Milan and among the ancient Greeks similar aids to oratory were credited to Zeus and Plato. Isidore had two brothers and a sister and all four of them have been canonised, an unequalled record. (Incidentally, they were not Goths, but members of a Hispano-Roman family from Cartagena.) Isidore was an ardent supporter of the Teutonic myth that sees superiority in unity of blood, leadership and religion. This led him to encourage persecution of the Jews, in defiance of Pope Gregory the Great, but it is doubtful whether he would have countenanced the vicious forms that it took after his death. A few Spanish historians perpetuate the story that the enslavement of the Jews was the result, rather than the cause, of their plotting with the Moslems and with their fellow-Jews of North Africa, to procure the downfall of the Visigoths. We shall see that these last were quite capable of effecting their own extinction.

Their downfall was sudden and complete; it revealed at the same time the expansive force of the fighting creed of Islam and the rottenness of the Visigothic state. Witiza, who died in 710, had been made joint-ruler with his royal father; he in turn tried to do the same for his own son, but now the nobles, keen supporters of

Germanic election versus heredity, declared a preference for their choice, Roderick who, contrary to what was alleged by his opponents, had royal ancestry. Civil war broke out on Witiza's death. The governor of Ceuta, on the African side of the Straits of Gibraltar, was a supporter of the Witiza faction. We know very little about him; from Christian sources we know him as Count Julian though Arabic sources give his name as Olban. We do not even know whether Ceuta was Spanish or Byzantine or independent, nor whether Julian was a Visigoth, a Byzantine Greek or a Berber, though there is a strong suspicion that he belonged to the Gomer division of that nation. But we do know that Julian formally placed Ceuta under the protection of Musa, Moslem governor of North Africa, and inspired him with the idea of invading Spain.

The tale of Julian's daughter Florinda is equally uncertain. The legend of her seduction was mentioned in our survey of Toledo; we can at least be sure that if Julian did send a daughter to "finishing school" in the royal household of Toledo, and if she was there seduced by the king, it was by Witiza, as stated by all Christian sources, and not by Roderick, as believed by Arab historians, and also by Sir Walter Scott. Her other name, La Cava, simply derives from a rude Arabic word. The facts and dates that are beyond question are few: Julian made his submission to Musa in October, 709 and thereafter paid tribute. Roderick was not elected king until 710. In July of that year, Musa's lieutenant Tarik sent a Berber called Tarif (how confusing these names can be!) on a reconnaissance of the Spanish coast. The picturesque town of Tarifa keeps the raider's memory alive, as Gibraltar (Gebel Tarik) does that of his master. The distance from Tarifa to the African coast is short. The expedition was a success and Tarif returned with a notable amount of booty, among which the Spanish females particularly aroused Musa's interest.

Next year, 711, Roderick was in the north, suppressing one of many Basque revolts,[7] when news was brought that Tarik had landed with a larger force. He hurried south, summoned the nobles to bring aid and went out to meet the invaders. With singular stupidity he entrusted both wings of his army to Witiza's sons or brothers (their relationship is obscure) and their supporters, and prepared to do battle near the town of Medina Sidonia. On the last night some of his noble lieutenants conferred and the following account is given of the minutes, as it were, of the meeting. "This son of the bad woman has made himself master of our kingdom without being of royal blood (!) . . . Those people (i.e. the Moslems) don't want to establish themselves in our country; all they want is loot; once they have this they'll go away and leave us alone. Let us run away during the battle and the son of the bad woman will be defeated."[8] It does not need a college education to give a more colloquial rendering of the phrase *hijo de la mala mujer*.

And that was the end of Visigothic Spain. Even if the story is untrue it is an interesting ancestor of the favourite "stab-in-the-back" and "Nous sommes trahis" of the Visigoths' distant blood relations. To their shame let it be stated that one of Witiza's treacherous sons or brothers, Oppas, was archbishop of Seville, an unworthy successor to the sainted Isidore; that many Visigothic nobles continued to live on their vast country estates, allegedly by previous agreement with the invaders;[9] and that Visigothic females, such as Roderick's widow, willingly married high-ranking Moslems and adopted their religion. One of Witiza's grand-daughters, Sara, survived her first Arab husband and married a second. By these she produced some of the aristocratic clans of Al-Andalus, as the Moslems called their part of Spain.

I have given these details at some length as I want to emphasise that the assimilation of the Visigothic nobility into the people of Spain was superficial, whatever may have been their relation to the Moslem conquerors. You may have inferred as much by comparing their behaviour with that of the Spaniards of Saguntum and Numantia. Yet the legend of Gothic ancestors continues to obsess the Spaniard. It has been blamed for his pride, his stubbornness, even his aversion from manual labour; those who read my comments on the Celts and Iberians will know better. I myself should be prouder of Hispano-Roman than of Visigothic ancestry.

A final note. Until recently small numbers of a strange people lived in ghettoes in Spanish and French Navarre. In Arizcún, a few miles from the frontier, they may still be found, pale, blond, broad-cheeked and blue-eyed. Here they are called Agotes, in France Cagots, a name believed to mean "Dogs of Goths". Some say they are the fugitives of the Visigothic allies of the Moslems defeated at Poitiers by Charles Martel; others that they fled from the ferocious Albigensian crusade of Simon de Montfort in

Languedoc. For centuries they have been treated worse than Jews, segregated within the church and outside. They were believed to transmit leprosy, brought by crusading ancestors from the Holy Land; the truth is that they have a hereditary skin disease, exaggerated by intermarriage, which crops up even among those of their descendants who emigrated as far away as America. Today they are no longer shunned, nor fobbed off with an abbreviated litany on Sundays, nor forced to use a separate stoup of holy water. But they are still primitive and shy. Are these the last poor relics of a master race?

An impression of Gibraltar as seen from the African coast sketched in the early nineteenth century.

The Capilla Muzárabe in the Cathedral at Córdoba.

CHAPTER TWO

The Coming of Islam

There were hundreds of Moslems who helped to build the splendid civilisation of Islamic Spain and whose names survive. But by selecting only a few we gain an idea of their lives, their times and, of greater interest, their ethics.

First, let us dispose of some common fallacies. When we speak of the Moors, to whom do we refer? The name is derived from the area region of North Africa called Mauretania, whose inhabitants were not dark-skinned with negroid features; in fact not swarthy at all. "Of mixed Berber and Arab blood", says the dictionary, in defining the Moors. If this is accepted, then the conquerors of Spain were certainly not Moors, for the Arabs had conquered the land of the Berbers only some ten years before the invasion, allowing insufficient time for a conquering generation of mixed blood. The Berbers were a fair-skinned race; dark skins would not appear in Spain until Arab rulers imported Negro bodyguards and later waves of Berbers brought whole regiments of Ghanaians and convoys of Negro concubines.

An irritating solecism is the use of the word "Crescent" to connote Islam and its followers. That emblem was taken from the Byzantines by the Turks in the fifteenth century; it was not seen during the Islamic conquest of Spain, and the Reconquest, even when it was actuated by religious considerations, should not be described as "the struggle between the Cross and the Crescent".

Few writers reflect that the invaders were soldiers. They brought no women but they fathered large families. Hence they must have, and in fact are known to have, married Spanish women, as did many of their descendants. The inevitable result was that later generations, say the eighth or ninth, had no more than a trace of the invader in their ancestry. Among the first ten emirs six were blond and blue-eyed, and another two habitually dyed their beard and hair with henna, so that we are ignorant of their original colouring. Furthermore, mixed marriages were not one-sided; Christian royal and noble houses, at least before the year 1000, were often gratified to marry into the Moslem aristocracy. The "Moors" who were eventually forced to leave their Spanish homes were in most cases indistinguishable from their Spanish conquerors. Even in the late sixteenth century, when Cervantes was a prisoner of the Moors, their women seem to have had the whitest hands. So if we want to make mental pictures of much that I shall recount, we must start by abolishing the vision of "blackamoors".

The last fallacy is the belief that Islamic conquest entailed the choice between conversion and death. So far is this form the truth that Moslem commanders were careful to spare as many Christians and Jews, whom they called "People of the Book", as possible, even if it meant an elastic interpretation of the Prophet's commands. The reason was simple: converts to Islam were exempt from taxation and those who declined to become *muladíes* were the sole source of the poll-tax. The majority had little objection to becoming Moslems, possibly for this reason, but the staunch Mozarabs and Jews were allowed freedom of worhsip under their chosen religious leaders and played an important part in the history of Spanish art, and indeed of Spain itself.

The rest of this chapter attempts to sum up the story of the Islamic conquest as reflected in the lives of two Moslems.

MUSA IBN NUSAIR. The world of Islam was still ruled from a central authority, the Caliph or successor of the Prophet. The House of the Omayyads had successfully disputed the leadership with two other families descended from the Prophet, the Fatimids and the Abbassids. Unpopular everywhere except in Syria, they successfully directed the expansion of the new empire from their home in Damascus. Musa was one their most successful lieutenants and a born conqueror. After an outstanding career in the East, he was made governor of North Africa, where he completed the

The fortress at Almuñecar.

conquest of what is now Morocco. Ceuta was the only city that had not fallen to him but in 709 Count Julian, perhaps feeling insecure because of Visigothic party politics, made his submission to Musa.

He was well over seventy, even allowing for the shorter Mohammedan year (254 days) but in spite of his age, his obesity and his asthma, Musa was still receptive to new ideas, expecially if they embraced booty or captive women. When Julian, mindful of Tarif's exploit and possibly with a personal interest in a successful outcome, suggested a raid on Spain, Musa requested permission from headquarters in Damascus. The Caliph forbade him to expose Moslems blindly to the hazards of a sea passage. "That's quite in order, Commander of the Faithful." was Musa's reply, "I'll just send my freed man Tarik with the Berbers. If they win we'll profit by their victory; if they die we shall have come to no harm".

The first force of 7,000 Berbers was accordingly ferried over in several trips by four ships. Then reinforcements came and after the rout of the Visigoths, in July 712, Musa arrived with 8,000 Syrians. He was filled with rancour against his former slave, jealous of his splendid success and envious of the booty he had taken. So when Musa landed exactly a year after Tarik, Count Julian and various Visigothic nobles offered to show him areas untouched by Tarik where plunder would be plentiful. And so, guided by treacherous Goths, tolerated by Spaniards and welcomed by Jews, who saw in him the means of delivery from persecution, Musa broke new ground with little effort. A few cities refused to surrender; significantly, they were those which had resisted the Visigoths three centuries earlier, a sign that the old spirit was still alive. He took Medina Sidonia, then found Carmona more difficult; but his Visigothic fifth column, pretending to be refugees, were admitted and the same night opened the east gates, called the Gate of Córdoba. Seville resisted for some months, as did Mérida. The chronicle tells us that the Christian peace envoys from Mérida saw Musa's beard change from grey to henna-red, and then to the black of *reng*, on successive days, in preparation for the Feast of Fitr at the end of Ramadan. They were so astonished that they attributed the rapid changes to supernatural powers and counselled unconditional surrender.

Nothing he found in the way of loot could have equalled the Table of Solomon which Tarik had taken in Almeida, near

The coast of North Africa looms continuously across the Straits of Gibraltar from Tarifa in Spain.

Guadalajara. It had been one of the many costly wedding presents given to Galla Placidia three hundred years earlier; a likely enough story, for Titus had removed the treasures of Jerusalem to Rome, and Alaric with his Visigoths had sacked Rome before coming to Spain. The rest of the Jerusalem temple furniture was taken by the Vandals when they sacked Rome some fifty years later. The table was alleged to be made from a single piece of solid emerald (historians think green glass more likely) and the Arabs, who ascribed every work of outstanding quality to King Solomon, made no exception here. According to other legends the invaders found a hoard of twenty-four or more gold diadems in Toledo. Last century's discovery of the Visigothic votive crowns of Guarrazar gives the story unexpected support.

When Tarik rode out to meet his commander-in-chief and respectfully dismounted to greet him, all he got from Musa was a cut over the head with his whip and a demand for all the booty he had taken – including the table. Somewhere along the line a leg had been broken off; Musa accused Tarik of the theft and later himself became suspect, perhaps because he had a replacement made, of gold and pearls. At all events he was summoned to

The Gateway of Carmona.

Damascus by the Caliph al-Walid. On his arrival, laden with treasure, he found al-Walid dying and the successor Suleiman took an oath to crucify Musa, for reasons now unknown. I suspect that each chief was suspicious of his subordinate, probably with justification. One inevitably thinks of Gibbon's, "Philip . . . was an Arab by birth, and consequently, in the earlier part of his life, a robber by profession".[1]

Musa was finally spared through the intercession of an old friend at court. Old, paunchy and asthmatic, he had been exposed to the fierce heat of the Syrian summer throughout the day, but when released from the torment and brought before the Caliph, it was the old warrior who laid down the conditions under which he would accept his master's sentence. One condition not granted was that Musa should have the disposal of Tarik's person and property. Does this give us a clue to the cause of Musa's downfall? Had Tarik told tales of embezzlement, of Musa witholding the caliph's 20 per cent share of all booty? Did Solomon's Table, even with the new leg, fall short of expectations? Was Suleiman furious because Musa had arrived just before al-Walid's death, and he himself might therefore be deprived of the caliphal percentage? Whatever the cause, and some of the suggestions appear to be inconsistent, Musa's fall was sudden and complete. He survived it by no more than a year and died at the age of eighty, leaving a military record seldom surpassed. For forty years, he boasted, he had never sustained a defeat.

His son Abd al-Aziz, having married Roderick's widow, directed the campaign of expansion. He captured the towns of León and Astorga and recruited new warriors from the ranks of the Spaniards, as well as Visigothic allies. He made Seville his headquarters and was living there in 716, in the palace next to the Mosque of Robina,[2] when he was assassinated at the Caliph Suleiman's orders; thus he hardly outlived his father.

Though Musa and his son were dead, the impetus they had given to Islam in Europe continued. The Visigothic state had included parts of France so the Moslems also crossed the Pyrenees. Narbonne was occupied in 719, and by 732 their raiders had taken Nîmes, Carcassonne and Bordeaux. But in the same year they and their renegade Visigothic allies were soundly beaten between Tours and Poitiers by Charles Martel the Frank. The defeat was not so decisive as we are told. The invaders were after loot, not

land, for they took over the estates of only those inhabitants who
had fled. As Montgomery Watt stresses,[3] Islam was a way of
religion of townspeople; no settled country folk could have
tolerated a calendar in which seasons fell in different months from
year to year. That is why the fertile country of the central Spanish
plateau was assigned to the Berbers, who were also defrauded of
their share of the booty; the Arabs congregated principally in the
towns.

Another event occurred probably in 722, which would
ultimately decide the fate of Islam in Spain, Cantabrian mountaineers, possibly combining with Visigothic refugees, resisted the
invaders and this paltry but determined force is credited with the
victory of Covadonga, to which we shall return.

ABDERRAHMAN I.[4] If the Spaniards are by nature unable to
live in harmony, the Moslem invaders were no better. Arab tribes
were in almost continuous dissension, new settlers were humiliated
by veteran invaders, Yemenites quarrelled with Syrians, Arabs
with Berbers, town dwellers with countrymen. Nevertheless, the
greater part of Spain and the fertile south of France were in their
hands for over a generation and their eventual expulsion took nine
hundred years to achieve. Shortly after the conquest the Berbers
complained of the treatment they were receiving; their new lands
were no better than those they had left in Africa and their share of
plunder patently a fraud. To add to their annoyance, they had the
task of defending the frontiers of al-Andalus against the Christian
states that were forming in the Cantabrians and Pyrenees. Perhaps
the Berbers would have been satisfied with complaints and
demonstrations had not famine struck in 750. That year marked
their return to Africa, speeded no doubt by the increasing
numbers of Arab reinforcements. For in 741 a force of 7,000
Syrian cavalry, under a commander named Balch, was defeated in
battle in Morocco then fled to Ceuta and was besieged there.
Fortunately for them the Arab governor in Spain needed help, so
the *junds*, as Syrian feudal tenants were called, agreed to abandon
Ceuta, come to Spain and fight the disaffected Berbers. Balch was
killed in battle but his men, having disposed of the rebels, settled
happily in their new fiefs.

Meanwhile Arab discord had come to a head in the East. The
Omayyad dynasty was surrounded by enemies, their victims were

promoted to saints and anti-caliphs were set up, anticipating (or perhaps initiating) the schisms of the Catholic Church. After years of alternate rebellion and oppression the last Omayyad caliph was defeated by the Abbassids, whose black banner now prevailed over the white. Fleeing from Iraq he was pursued relentlessly and run to earth after six months in Upper Egypt, where he was struck down. But eastern revolts cannot be counted as successful if only the tyrant is slain; his relatives fled to their estates, where most were hunted down. One was captured had a hand and a foot amputated and was paraded through the towns of Syria until he died behind a crier who proclaimed; "This is the best warrior of the Omayyads". Then an amnesty was declared, safe conducts were given and about eighty of the Omayyad clan were celebrating the end of hostilities when their Abbassid hosts had them clubbed to death during the feast, spread a carpet over the corpses and finished their meal.

Of the few who rightly distrusted the Abbassid invitation to dinner, only one male, Abderrahman, eventually survived. As a grandson in the direct line of the caliphs he was eagerly sought and his escape entailed swimming the Euphrates with his thirteen year-old brother. The Abbassid pursuers invited them to return, promising that they had nothing to fear. His brother did so and was murdered out of hand. Later, Abderrahman secretly crossed the isthmus of Suez and survived the designs of a treacherous governor of Tunis. His mother had been a Berber captive, so he found safety among the members of her tribe. His hazardous journey took four years, but surviving the attentions of false friends and envious enemies, he at length settled between Taza and the River Muluya, a little east of Fez.

In Spain, news of a surviving Omayyad excited partisans of that faction, such as the *junds*, as well as other disaffected communities, of which Spain has never had a shortage. For things had been going badly since the great famine of 750. Thanks to his friend and servant, the faithful Badr, the prince was invited to Spain and a small but welcome sum sent with the invitation. The money was used to compensate his Berber hosts and for travelling expenses and in August 755, Abderrahman landed at what is now the little coastal resort of Almuñecar.

In less than a year he had collected a large following and was marching on Córdoba, capital of the Abbassid governor. For some days the opposing armies were separated by the river Guadalquivir; then Abderrahman, agreeing to the *wali*'s terms, gained time to get his troops across the river at night. In the next day's battle his despicable behaviour was rewarded with victory. He restrained his troops from sacking Córdoba and proved to be such a stern disciplinarian that they tried to assassinate him. To celebrate his victory he had himself proclaimed, not a mere *wali* (governor), like his defeated opponent, but emir, a distinguished rank for a man of twenty-five. From now on the Omayyads would rule in Spain as independent commanders or emirs — until, that is, they set themselves up as Caliphs, or successors of the Prophet.

But Abderrahman's task was only beginning. From 756 to 788 his reign was one long battle against bloody uprisings and murderous intrigues. Both his own troops and the kinsmen he had invited to Spain were unreliable and he was finally forced to recruit an army of Berber mercenaries, who proved more faithful. For five years their wages and equipment were levied from the Mozarabs in what became the Province of Granada, possibly as a punishment for their support of the Abbassid governor. For the Abbassids were not ready to give up their Spanish territory. In 763 an agitator arrived with money from Baghdad, found enthusiastic support among Abderrahman's enemies — and friends — raised the black flag and marched on Córdoba. The emir took refuge behind the Roman-Visigothic-Arab gates of Carmona and struck back two months later. Seven thousand rebel heads were collected after the battle and those of Abbassid agents carefully pickled. Then their names were written on parchment labels and hung from their ears. The heads, with an account of the insurrection, were wrapped in the black flag, put in a sack and given to a merchant with instructions to leave it secretly in the market place of Kairwan. This was duly done and it was thus that the Caliph in Baghdad learned the result of his plot. His comment was both sensible and pious: "Thanks be to Allah," he exclaimed, "that he has put the sea between me and this devil."

Apart from showing his strength, a Moslem ruler was expected to set an example of piety and the emir did this by buying from the Christians of Córdoba the half of their cathedral which they had retained, and building on the site the first portion of the world-famous mosque.

Even to those who have never heard of Abderrahman, one

episode that occurred during his emirate should be familiar. Charlemagne had enlarged and secured his vast empire by 778. Though the Saxons were still troublesome he was ready to listen to the proposal of treacherous Arabs, especially the governor of Zaragoza. Persuaded or bribed by an Abbassid agent, the governor rebelled against Abderrahman and went to Paderborn to meet Charlemagne. The latter possibly dreamed of incorporating in his own empire the long defunct empire of the Visigoths. He advanced through the Pyrenees, received the submission of the Basques of Pamplona and marched to Zaragoza. The gates were to be open to receive him, but the traitor's deputy, finding command sweeter then locum tenancy, kept them closed. The Franks settled down to a siege, but a Saxon rebellion forced them to return home with all speed.

It was while they were retreating through Roncesvalles that the rearguard, under the paladin Roland, was annihilated by the Basques, who obtained their victory economically by rolling boulders down the sides of the pass. Though the Basques, probably after booty, were the prime movers, there may be some truth in the old, discarded tale that Roland died fighting the Moslems. For Charlemagne took with him, as a prisoner, the treacherous governor of Zaragoza, and an Arab chronicle describes how the latter's two sons joined forces with the Basques and rescued their father at Roncesvalles. We learn with satisfaction that he was soon murdered in Zaragoza by his deputy. Thus there may be a germ of truth in the Song of Roland, where the "paynim ' are described as the enemy.

But where the epic exchanges exaggeration for fabrication is in Charlemagne's statement, "Never to Paynims may I show love or peace".[5] One of the more reliable Arab historians, Ibn Hayyan, wrote, "The king of the Franks, Charles, powerful ruler of that nation, corresponded with 'Abd al-Rahman I, after having kept up hostile relations for a certain time. Taking into account that the emir was endowed with truly notable energy and bravery, he tried to tempt him by the offer of a matrimonial alliance and a truce. 'Abd al-Rahman gave a favourable answer respecting the truce; but the matrimonial alliance did not take place".[6]

It is impossible to be dogmatic about attitudes and policies after twelve centuries, but it is certain that Charlemagne exchanged cordial greetings, after Abderrahman's death, with his dynastic

The entrance to the town of Carmona (nineteenth-century drawing).

enemy, the Abbassid Caliph Haroun al-Rashid; it is even said that the latter sent Charlemagne exotic presents and with them the keys of Jerusalem. It is also likely that Charlemagne made peace overtures to Abderrahman's grandson and second successor, al-Haqem I.

The imagination kindles when it considers the career of Abderrahman. For years a hunted refugee, then the clandestine guest of a savage tribe; pretender to one of his persecutor's richest lands, invader, fighter, governor and self-made commander-in-chief, eventually to be treated as an equal by Charlemagne, the

first Holy Roman Emperor. Thirty years of rule, always anticipating treachery, zealously preserving his frontiers, fighting rebel-
lions year after year. He founded a dynasty which was to rule
Spain for over two hundred years and preside over one of the
world's great cultural advances. Is it not fortunate that we have
this pen portrait of him?

Tall, blond and one-eyed. Lean cheeks and hair parted to fall in
curls on either side. Athletic and a master of the sword, but
equally deadly drawing the bow on horseback. The historian
al-Razi wrote, "His speech was ready and elegant and he could
compose poetry; suave, educated, resolute, quick to hunt down
rebels, he never rested or gave himself up to relaxation for long.
He never withdrew from the conduct of affairs and trusted only in
his own intellect. He joined fierce courage with exceptional
prudence. They compared him with al-Mansur, the Abbassid
caliph, in the firmness of his will, in his energy and his inflexible
rule."

And now for al-Mansur himself, Abderrahman's mortal enemy.
He once asked his courtiers, "Who is the hawk of the
Quraish?"[7]

"The Commander of the Faithful . . ." ventured the flatterers.

"No", said the Caliph, and "No" to every other suggestion.
Then he explained.

"Abd al-Rahman ibn Mwawiya who, escaping lance and sword
by his wits, passed through the desert, crossed the sea, entered a
land of pagans, founded cities, built up armies and organised a
state, where all was anarchy before, by good administration and
firmness of character." Then, after detailing the good fortune that
helped his own rise and that of other caliphs, he continued, "but
Abd al-Rahman was alone, with no help other than his intelligence, with no companion but his inflexible will."[8]

The Rocio, a time-honoured Easter tradition when Andalusian couples don their traditional finery and ride into Seville to participate in the world-famous Sevillian feria. Both the men's and the women's costumes retain many moorish elements. (Front cover, *Feature-Pix*)

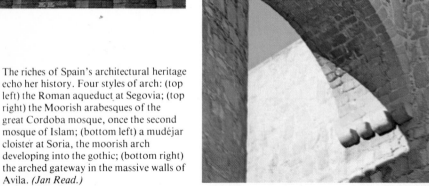

The riches of Spain's architectural heritage
echo her history. Four styles of arch: (top
left) the Roman aqueduct at Segovia; (top
right) the Moorish arabesques of the
great Cordoba mosque, once the second
mosque of Islam; (bottom left) a mudéjar
cloister at Soria, the moorish arch
developing into the gothic; (bottom right)
the arched gateway in the massive walls of
Avila. *(Jan Read.)*

Castles in Spain. The Segovia castle is one dramatic example of hundreds of magnificent stone fortresses in Spain. (Back cover.)

Glazed Arab tiles inside the Alcázar in Seville. Arab artists initiated the great tradition of glazed tilings for homes and public buildings in Spain. *(Jan Read)*

A traditional tiled kitchen from the Palace of the Marquis of dos Aguas in Valencia. *(Jan Read)*

CHAPTER THREE

Emirs, Caliphs and their Downfall

Having followed the career of the bloody, bold and resolute Abderrahman I let us summarise events over the next century — the ninth.

We begin with a bauble of more intrinsic value than most, the Girdle of Zobeida; it was to play its part in the history of Spain for a thousand years. For his favourite wife, of whose facial and other attractions we may read in the uninhibited pages of "The Arabian Nights", the Caliph Haroun al-Rashid ordered a jewelled girdle. So numerous and fine were the gems that the girdle became legendary even during its owner's life-time. It seems, from the rhapsodies of contemporary poets, to have been a band solidly encrusted with pearls and diamonds; at intervals alternate rubies and sapphires glowed with vivid colour. The clasp, flanked by two great emeralds, was of the finest workmanship, cunningly made to represent a scorpion, whose curved tail and sting engaged with its corresponding jewelled staple. After the deaths of Haroun and Zobeida, their son Amin became Caliph, his weakness leading inevitably to his assassination in 813.

His treasure, and with it his mother's girdle, was rescued and taken to Spain with a guard of gigantic negroes. The Emir of the West eagerly bought it and it is said to have sparkled in the moonlight of al-Andalus, on many an enchanted night, on the swaying hips of the most beautiful women of the Western world.

Meanwhile the frontiers of Islamic Spain, always unstable, underwent important changes. In the north the city of Gerona

. The Castle at Marbella.

handed itself over to Charlemagne's French troops, probably because its own unscrupulous Moslem governors were harder to endure than a set of unbelievers. In 801 Charlemagne occupied and retained Barcelona. Thus a large part of what is now Catalonia was under French influence at an early date; the variety of the Romance tongue in use here was Languedoc, nearer to French than to Castilian or other Spanish forms, as indeed modern Catalan continues to be.

Back in 750, when the Berber garrisons were returning to Africa, all the plain north of the River Duero was deserted, and it was not long before the kings of the little state of Asturias cautiously took over sections of the flat land. León and Astorga were the most important occupations — it would be too much to call them reconquests — and the ninth and tenth centuries saw the acquisition of more land. Alfonso III of Asturias (shortly to be called the Kingdom of León) was especially successful. He was helped by good timing, for the Moslems were usually otherwise occupied when he took over new territory, and by an opportune episode of persecution of the Mozarabs; as these fled north they were usefully settled in the recently conquered, unpopulated land.

Distracted by frequent revolts and by incursions from each frontier and on every coast, the emirs found it convenient to maintain deserted border provinces, or marches. The upper was

The ruins of the fortress at Gormaz.

controlled from Zaragoza, whose governor soon became semi-independent; the middle comprised all the area north of Toledo, on which important city it was based, and the lower, governed from Mérida, roughly embraced all the land between the Guadiana and Duero rivers. But in addition to these frontiers the coast had to be protected. In 844 a chain of forts and towers was built to keep out the Vikings, who nevertheless managed to sail up the Guadalquivir and destroy Seville. They were a menace, not only to the Atlantic, but to the Mediterranean coasts; scarcely had they moved on to more promising shores than the Fatimids began their westward expansion along the fertile strip of North Africa and caused serious concern to the Omayyads of Spain. Their memory is kept alive by such defences as the castle in the popular seaside town of Marbella.

During this time changes in the population of Spain were striking. Arab immigration was slowing down; Berbers and negroes, male and female, were brought in to swell the numbers of army and harem. So-called Slavs were imported from northern and eastern Europe, those who escaped the castraters of Verdun being employed as soldiers. Eventually the army became a permanent organisation, consisting mainly of Berbers and Slavs but containing also a good number of Mozarabs and even foreign Christian allies. For the crusading spirit was still in the future; at least up to the year 1000 Christians fought for Moslem employers, and Moslems for Christian, with no thought of disloyalty to country or creed. From time to time the emirs temporarily swelled their ranks by declaring a *jehad*, or holy war, and used the resulting volunteers for the usual type of foray. When they cried "Wolf!" too often, enthusiasm for holy wars dwindled.

The ninth century was a period of strange adventures by exiled Spaniards. A whole suburb of Córdoba revolted in the second decade; subdued after considerable bloodshed they were driven out of their homes and decided to seek their fortunes elsewhere. Most were *muladíes* (Christian converts) but Berbers also joined them. They took ship and made for Alexandria, which they captured and occupied for ten years, as an independent state. Persuaded to leave, they landed in Crete, conquered the whole island from the Byzantines and stayed from 827 until 961, under the dynasty that began with the Cordoban Abu Hafs Omar al-Ballutí, living by piracy. In 840 the Emperor of Byzantium sent an embassy to Córdoba requesting the emir's help in rooting out this pirates' nest but assistance was politely witheld.

The venturesome spirit of both Moslem and Mozarabic pirates deserves the adjective "intrepid". One expedition founded a colony at Fraxinetum, today La Garde-Freinet on the Montagnes des Maures, inland from St Tropez. There they remained, an island of "Moors" (Maures) in the heart of Provence; and they, or perhaps Spanish Moslem forces, raided through northern Italy, to Switzerland (Pontresina is only *pons Saracinorum*, "the Saracens' bridge") and made several sorties up the Rhône. One band of these scoundrels captured Roland, Bishop of Arles, who had sallied forth armed to do battle. On the point of being ransomed the poor prelate died, but the pirates were not thus to be cheated: they dressed the late bishop in his vestments, sat his corpse in a chair on the sands and made sure that the ransom was in their hands before they let his rejoicing flock approach near enough to detect the fraud.

Inside al-Andalus organisation kept up with the pursuit of pleasure and culture, the two often being synonymous. Supervision of town life was in the hands of a judicial department, which included the *sahib al-madina* (town governor) and *sahib al-suq* (market master), both of whom were able to order the death penalty. The latter survives in the Spanish *zabazoque*. Elsewhere life was made safer by castles, such as that of Gormaz, and more agreeable with aqueducts, of which sections, such as that near Ronda, still remain.

Once settled in Spain the Moslems gradually shed the more restrictive features of their religion, beginning usually, by drinking wine. Hardly had the Prophet expired when attempts were made to circumvent his prohibition of wine, expressly laid down in the Sura of the Cow. As the Koran states that in both wine and gambling there is great sin and also some things of use unto men, an enthusiastic school of interpretation advised only moderation; naturally their ideas took root in the fertile soil of Andalucía, whose inhabitants outdid each other in the practice of moderation until the magistrates' courts felt the strain. Inevitably the law became more lenient, especially as the Prophet had died without detailing the punishment for drunkenness, an oversight which proved very useful to sympathetic magistrates. Al-Khushani, to whom I am indebted for many anecdotes, relates how a Córdoban judge ordered the arrest of a drunken man in the street; hearing this the offender called out, "Come and take me yourself, Judge. And if you touch me, by God I'll give you a clout you'll remember!" At which the judge made a detour down a side street, remarking to his companion, "Thank God we let him off; I believe he's capable of doing it."[1]

But life was not one long orgy. The ninth century saw the beginning of a cultural revival that put Córdoba far ahead of Byzantium and of the efforts of Charlemagne who, incidentally, drew much of his inspiration from Spain. Sciences and crafts arrived from the East, astronomy from India, poetry and philosophy from Baghdad; local talent was not wanting either and one of the despised Berbers proved his genius in many fields. Abbas Ibn Firnas not only absorbed what others had invented but solved riddles and problems that baffled the local sages. With home-made instruments he invented a new method of working glass, and with it produced a complicated model of the universe. He is best remembered for his aeronautical experiments; using a glider made of feathers he took off from the hills behind Córdoba and managed to cover a good distance before landing gently enough to break only a leg.

But Ziryab was the man of the century. The nick-name means blackbird and was given him because of his dark complexion; his own name is too long to set out here. Educated by the court musician of Baghdad, he showed such genius that Haroun al-Rashid was impressed and the teacher became jealous of his pupil; scenting danger Ziryab made off westward and was welcomed in Spain, where he revolutionised not only music, but the whole standard of living. As an arbiter of elegance he was a worthy successor of Petronius and forerunner of Beau Brummel. He modified musical instruments, introduced glassware for the table, beauty parlours and their methods, summer and winter clothing fashions and a science of gastronomy. The cuisine of Baghdad was far more subtle that that of al-Andalus and Ziryab was able to reproduce it, teaching the proper sequence of courses, literally from soup to nuts, to replace the disorganised meals that were current.

In following the fortunes of foreigners, we must not lose sight of the Spaniards themselves. The majority had, as I have said, converted to Islam and, as time went on, they took the name and genealogy of their patron so that they could eventually pass themselves off as Arabs, even when independent of their master. The Mozarabs were regarded as inferior to Moslems, whom they were forbidden to employ, but they were allowed their own churches and laws.

When the monk John of Görtz went to the court of Abderrahman III in the year 953, as ambassador of the Emperor Otto, he had a talk with one of the Mozarab bishops. The latter excused his subservience to the Moslems, pointing out that the Bible enjoined obedience to established authority and that the Moslems were not such terrible people, in that they permitted Christian worship and shared the Christians' loathing of the Jews. It was by then quite usual for the Mozarabs to be circumcised and was even compulsory for a time, so the poor bishop had to make his excuses for personal participation in the custom, much to the disgust of John, who fired a text from Galatians (5:2) at him.

In return for their contributions to agriculture and architecture, the Mozarabs derived and handed on the benefit of scientific knowledge elaborated by Arabs and Jews, so that at least one staunch Christian lamented their zealous study of Arabic books. They were well supported from outside Spain. In the tenth century, for instance, the monk Gerbert spent some years in Córdoba, later ascending to the chair of St Peter as Sylvester II.

Daniel Morley, though he had studied at Oxford and Paris, was among those who came to Toledo to learn Arabic, so that he could study mathematics. The English Benedictine Abelard, well known in the history of philosophy, also came to Toledo, where he learned enough Arabic to translate the *Elements* of Euclid. A constant stream of scholars flowed to the great centres of Moslem learning, whence they conveyed to the rest of Europe not only the scientific achievements of the Arab world, but the older treasures of Greek civilisation, kept alive by Moslem and Jewish scholars.

But this is anticipating and perhaps presenting too rosy a picture. The Mozarabs were well to the fore in objecting, openly or secretly, to the type of government that prevailed. In 851, in spite of the advice of their synod, an epidemic of voluntary martyrdom reached its peak in Córdoba. Christians, usually monks or juveniles, made sure of their fate by insulting the religion of their masters, often by spitting on the Koran. Even had the emir or judges been inclined to mercy, the law did not permit them to exercise it and the death of the judge was decreed if the offender had not been executed on the day he was arrested. Their bishop, Eulogius, was long spared but in 859 he made it impossible for the authorities to overlook his open blasphemy; he remained obdurate during his trial and promptly followed his flock to Heaven, where he presumably heard the news of his canonisation. The persecution which these events aroused caused a mass emigration of Mozarabs, some to France but the majority to Christian Spain; they formed another stream by which the West profited.

Though the authorities were constantly kept busy with revolts and frontier wars, their gravest concern was undoubtedly the threat of Omar Ibn Hafsun. This *muladí*, or rather grandson of a converted Christian, made his headquarters in Bobastro, in the mountains east of Ronda, gathered round him a band of desperadoes, conquered a large part of what is now Andalucía and, in short, made emirs and their generals look helpless. So marked was his success that other *muladíes* made themselves independent of Córdoba and set up courts like petty kings. This occurred in the second half of the ninth century, immediately after the epidemic of voluntary martyrdom at Córdoba. There is a legend that the Mozarabs contemplated rebellion and the invitation of Ibn Hafsun to the emirate; all that happened, however, is that a Mozarab notable and rogue (called Servando in the Romance language and

Ibn Hachchach in Arabic) turned traitor to the emir; he was hunted down and killed. Ibn Hafsun's state survived for over fifty years, thanks to the combined gifts of generalship and treachery. He anticipated many another *guerillero* by accepting bribes to enrol himself in the government forces — but only for as long as it suited him. He died in his bed and his sons carried on the struggle, hopeless though it was for the time when their father turned Christian and lost his Moslem supporters. The downfall of his independent state coincided with the most glorious period of Moslem rule in Spain.

ABDERRAHMAN III's reign of fifty years marked the zenith of Moslem power. The Christian states largely held back, internal peace was secured although, as ever in Arab communities, successful autocracy bred envy among the nobles. I have remarked that the Moslems of Spain were predominantly Spanish by descent and this is true of the new ruler too. His mother and his father's mother were both Basques of Navarre and similar heredity went back for many generations. His dark blue eyes, his red-gold hair and beard, as well as his character, were quite unlike our concept of the oriental. At twenty-one, when he came to the throne, he already showed moral and intellectual eminence. Ambitious but realistic, pious but tolerant, brilliant and decisive, he gained the respect of the intelligent and the affection of the simple. It is related that, on one occasion, only the earnest advice of the holy men prevented him from appointing a Mozarab Chief Justice of Córdoba.

With the death of Ibn Hafsun he found it easy to put down the rebellion in Andalucía, and to recover Badajoz and Toledo from other rebels. He sustained one clear-cut defeat, against Ramiro II of León, in 939. At Simancas the Christian king took advantage of a temporary slackening in the Moslem fighting spirit to pin the enemy between attackers and a deep fosse; the Moslems fled and Abderrahman was content to save his life and abandon his valuables. Anticipating Napoleon he sent an advance party home, announcing that he was safe and sound; he also had gibbets and crosses erected along the river bank at Córdoba, to hang and crucify three hundred of his officers for cowardice. Luckier than Napoleon, Abderrahman could leave his enemies to fight each other and soon re-established his ascendancy.

One is appalled by the savage punishment inflicted on his unfortunate scapegoats, and equally by the report that he had one of his own sons hanged before his eyes, when he was found to be implicated in a palace assassination plot. But the more we read of those days, the more readily we believe that such behaviour was compatible with lofty standards of morality.

His other external threat came from North Africa. The Abbassids were reduced to impotence, vainly trying to stem the pressure of Central Asiatic hordes. The Fatimids of North Africa took the opportunity of setting up as rival Caliphs and enlarged their territory, at the same time creating a powerful fleet, with which they were to sack Almería in 955, Abderrahman had designs on North Africa himself, establishing supremacy over Tunis and other cities between 947 and 951; furthermore the Spanish rebel Ibn Hafsun had sworn allegiance to the Fatimid caliph. Abderrahman had countered by having himself proclaimed Caliph at Córdoba, with the customary titles *emir al-muminin* ("Commander of the Faithful") and *al-Nasir li-din Allah* ("he who fights victoriously for the faith of Allah").[2] This was done in 929, so that one of his titles did not bear scrutiny ten years later at Simancas. Nevertheless, such was the discord between Christian kings that by 951 Abderrahman and his successors were recognised by León, Navarre, Castile and Barcelona. No formality this, for it entailed the payment of tribute and demolition of frontier fortresses. Incidentally, the story of the annual tribute of a hundred damsels is impure invention; true, Christian girls were popular, but many came voluntarily and others were sold to itinerant dealers by their parents. There was much intermarriage and the family tree of the Banu Qasi shows how close were the ties between that Arabic family and the House of Navarre, and between the latter and the Caliphs of Córdoba. One infers that there was little feeling of a religious war, at least on the Christian side, and none, at this stage, of a Reconquest, in the sense of recovering the whole Visigothic empire.

The climate of feeling is well reflected in the tale of Sancho the Fat and Ordoño the Bad. The former, rightful King of León, was superseded by Ordoño with no reasonable excuse. Sancho took refuge with his grandmother, Toda the Queen Regent of Navarre. She appealed to Abderrahman, perhaps on the grounds of kinship; the Caliph therefore sent his usual roving ambassador, the Jew

The aqueduct at Ronda.

One of the precipitous cliffs that made Ronda a natural fortress. (*Jan Read*)

Abu Yusuf Hasday ibn Shaprut, an outstanding linguist and a physician of repute. As Sancho's obesity could serve as an excuse for keeping him from the throne, he promised to prescribe; but he insisted that Sancho, his father the King of Navarre and his grandmother would have to come to Córdoba to do homage. The conditions were accepted, the journey made, homage offered, and Sancho lost enough weight to enable him to ride a horse again, so that he could enter León in fitting style when Abderrahman had captured it for him.

The next act took place after Abderrahman's death. His son al-Haqem II maintained the caliphal splendour in the palace of Medina Azzahra, built by his father. Ordoño the Bad came in his turn and asked for help in turning out Sancho the ex-Fat. His interview with the Caliph makes sickening reading: the prostrations, the kissing of the carpet, and of the hand; the backward withdrawal and the same procedure followed by his retinue. Then the flattery, the kneeling in thanks the second withdrawal with face rigidly to the throne; another genuflection in front of an empty chair in the ante-room, often used by the Caliph himself, the attempt to kiss the vizier's hand. Reconquest?

Before we leave Abderrahman III, at least a passing reference must be made to his fabulous palace-residence of Medina Azzahra. The story has been told often enough, sometimes accurately. The complex was built with the money bequeathed by a favourite concubine, to honour the next favourite, whose idea it was; the Caliph was even sufficiently infatuated to put her statue over the main gate. A terrible libel, for the Guardian of the Faith should have had nothing to do with graven images; but in this case the libel is also the truth and there is a record of the statue being demolished by order of a twelfth-century fanatic. Abderrahman III also towers over Spanish rulers, at least until Alfonso X in the thirteenth century, as a patron of arts and letters. His library was one of the largest in the world but it did not survive him long. He died in 961, after a reign of fifty Arabic years. Afterwards they found a paper on which he had noted "the days of my life on which I enjoyed pure pleasure and no worries were . . . . of . . . . month, of . . . . year". The total was fourteen.

ALMANZOR. His name was Abu 'Amir Muhammad Ibn Abi 'Amir al-Ma'afiri, but he is better known as al-Mansur, the Victorious. In

A portrait of Almanzor by
one of Spain's greatest
painters, Zurbaran.

the Christian chronicles the name was written Almanzor and it is
thus that we speak of him, even though he did not assume the title
until late in his career. He was the blackest-hearted, meanest-
minded villain that ever held Spain in his grasp; worse, he added
genius to ambition, cunning, ruthlessness and cruelty.

Born in 940, in the reign of Abderrahman III, he began his
career under al-Haqem II. He came of a good, middle-class family
of Yemeni Arabs and was exceptional in having an Arab mother
too; among his ancestors he numbered one of Tarik's officers. As a
young man he studied law and letters at Córdoba, where he is said
to have shown the first signs of his remorseless competitive spirit.
He became a scribe and his intelligence soon drew the attention of
a magistrate who recommended him to the vizier, al-Mushrafí.
Al-Haqem, in his late forties, became the father of an heir and,

though the boy soon died, the same concubine produced another son in 965. The *Umm walad*, as the privileged mother of a son was called, was now wealthy in her own right and it was desirable to find her and her son an administrator. Almanzor was the man.

The lucky mother was Basque who had been given the Arabic name Subh, meaning "Dawn", and is therefore often called Aurora by historians. In accordance with an old Baghdad custom she was given the male name of Cha'far when she became favourite; others, however, ascribe it to her habit of wearing men's clothes, possibly to accord with her master's sexual inclinations. There is no record of Almanzor's physical attraction and his ascendancy over Subh may be attributed to his subtlety. So blatant indeed were his attentions, not only to Princess Subh but to other inmates of the harem, that al-Haqem, whose interests were books and boys, is reported to have asked without rancour, "By what clever devices does this young man so attract my women that their hearts are his?"

In seven months Almanzor became director of the mint, in a year court treasurer and soon afterwards a judge of the Seville-Niebla circuit. On one occasion he survived the auditors' scrutiny by borrowing from a friend enough money to cover the deficit. He had now mounted the first two rungs of the ladder, the first through the vizier al-Mushrafí and the second, more literally, Princess Subh.

Such was the confidence placed in him by the Caliph that he was next sent to North Africa as quartermaster-general and paymaster to General Galib, a Slav and freedman from the days of Abderrahman III. From him Almanzor learned the art of war and, predictably, became more adept at it than his teacher. Al-Haqem died in 976 and Almanzor joined the Berber vizier Cha'far al-Mushrafí as regent for Hishem II, aged eleven, remaining administrator of the young Caliph's estate. He kept his influence over Subh and promised her that he would restore the frontiers of al-Andalus to their maximum. He was also given the important assignment of disposing of the late al-Haqem's brother, a harmless private person without designs on the throne. In spite of his protestations and entreaties, justified in an unworldly scholar, Almanzor left him to the stranglers.

Another of his activities had been the recruitment of a private army of Slavs and Berbers; with these he joined Galib in opposing his co-regent and benefactor al-Mushrafi. Their campaign was successful and Almanzor was appointed city commandant (*sahib al-madina*) over al-Mushrafí's son. Al-Mushrafí scented danger and tried to curry favour with Galib by pointing out that Almanzor and his friends were all Arabs and therefore hostile to non-Arab Moslems; to strengthen his position he asked for the hand of Galib's daughter. All appeared to be going smoothly and the menace of Almanzor receding, when al-Mushrafí was suddenly informed that the girl was married – to Almanzor.

Now al-Mushrafi, the old, all-powerful vizier crawled; he and his family were removed from their posts and heavily fined for embezzlement, Almanzor's old failing. For five years he took menial jobs while his enemy waited for him to die a natural death. When this became overdue Almanzor had him removed to prison and strangled. Thus perished the first rung of Almanzor's ladder. The second, Subh, was soon thrown over, but not before she had helped her lover in the corruption of her own son, the Caliph Hishem II. By 981 supreme power was vested in the career man, though Hishem, at the age of sixteen, remained nominal Caliph. His mother nursed her resentment for years, to no purpose. Her only memorial today is a plaque set in the bell tower of the Church of Santa Cruz in Écija, commemorating the gift of a fountain by *al-sayidda al-kubra*, the Great Princess.

To rival the caliphal palace-city of Medina, Azzahra Almanzor now built his own adminstrative palace, Medina Azzahira, "the brilliant city"; the name alone is enough to tell us how he defied the boy caliph and his mother. All the world now thronged to the new palace, and any who could help his career were made welcome. Today even its site is unknown. With a reorganised army of Berbers and Christian mercenaries and his gift for inspiring fear, Almanzor soon imposed order on what had become the lawless city of Córdoba. His popularity rose and was prejudiced only by mutterings about his lack of piety. He was too shrewd to allow such rumours to gain credence. In 981 he began a series of personally conducted campaigns against the Christian kingdoms. In twenty years he led over fifty such expeditions, without once suffering defeat. During the *jehad*, or holy war, as he called it, he sacked every Christian capital in Spain. So well indeed had Galib taught him that Almanzor was described as the most intrepid and fortunate warrior that his country had ever known.

In 987 he began building the fourth and largest extension to Córdoba's magnificent mosque, helping with his own hands, and he let it be known that, in conformity with the Koranic precept, he collected the dust that gathered on his face and clothes during his "holy" wars and saved it for his own funeral. The legend of the pious warrior was finally consummated when he led his army to Santiago de Compostela, the most sacred Christian shrine in western Europe; his force this time included, not only the usual Christian mercenaries, but free Christian allies from the north-west of Iberia. He destroyed the town and walls completely, sparing only the tomb of St James and its guardian monk.

A long line of captives trudged to Córdoba, carrying the smaller bells of the Cathedral for use in the Mosque as oil lamps. They also carried the gates of the city, destined for the ceiling of the new addition. Santiago the warrior saint and slayer of Moors, who had helped the Christians to victory so often, was himself helpless before the terrible Almanzor and his Christian allies. But that would have no lasting effect; in hagiology, as in Medicine, it is as difficult to lose a reputation as to gain one. Almanzor's deference to the religious conservatives was as thoroughly planned as one of his annual or biennial campaigns. He therefore joined the exclusive ranks of that special section of the damned, the quenchers of the torch. Like the Caliph Omar before him, and Cardinal Cisneros later, he ordered the destruction of thousands of books. From among those so lovingly collected by his first master Haqem II, he kept only those which treated of religion, medicine or related sciences; philosophy to the flames!

But what of Galib? It was not like Almanzor to avert his sinister glance from a friend who had helped him to success, even if it was his father-in-law. In 981 he forced a quarrel on the old man, who tried to save himself with the help of the Christian states of León, Castile and Navarre. The battle was fought at Vicente, near Medinaceli; all the valour and skill of the eighty-year-old general could not prevail against his brilliant and ever fortunate pupil. Galib's horse fell and killed him, while he was striving to come to grips with the "accursed hunchback", as he called his son-in-law. (This is the only reference we have to the latter's appearance.) Almanzor burst forth into loud thanks to Allah and from that day took the title by which we know him best.

Again he ravaged the lands of Galib's allies. Once more the loads of booty and the long files of captives made their way to Córdoba and now the market was so glutted with Christian slaves that a new low price was reached in the slump. In 984 King Sancho Garcés II of Pamplona gave him his daughter Abda in marriage. She duly obliged by producing a son, named Abderrahman Sanchuelo, a compliment to his Navarrese grandfather. When the latter came on a visit to Córdoba his grandson, though only eight, was vizier. Old Sancho Garcés knew enough to kiss the ground between the boy's hands, as they do in the "Arabian Nights", and then his foot.

Another Christian princess, daughter of Bermudo II of León, was offered and accepted as Almanzor's concubine. She at least had the spirit to tell her escort, "A nation should entrust its honour to its warriors' lances and not to its women's charms." She later achieved the status of wife. Don't imagine that this was anything like the fate that is worse than death. For example, a fairly reliable account from tenth-century Castile tells how a Count's wife fed his horse on bran only, so that it was sluggish in the next skirmish and its rider was killed. The story is credible because Spanish Christian knights in those days kept their war horse in the bedroom and its feeding was the wife's responsibility. And her reason? She wanted to become a member of Almanzor's harem. These cases were not exceptions; we know, for instance, that Teresa, sister of Alfonso V, married a Moslem "rebel" after Almanzor's death and became, for a time, "queen" of Toledo.

The story of Almanzor's defeat at Calatañazor (today only a fortified village) and subsequent death is a myth. He died apparently from natural causes, for "Allah heard his prayer to be summoned while pursuing the holy war." He was buried where he died, in Medinaceli, in a shroud spun by his daughters from material bought with the proceeds of his own patrimony. His son and heir, whom I shall call al-Muzaffar for short, himself poured the dust of the campaigns into his father's coffin and so Almanzor was buried in the odour of sanctity, a testimonial to the virtue of villainy, when accompanied by intelligence.

Like his father, Almanzor's son was *de facto* ruler of al-Andalus, but briefly, for he died at the age of thirty-three. During his six years of power he maintained the fiction of a Caliph in the person of Hishem II and kept at his court the customary throng of poets, astrologers and professional chess players. For the last time Islamic

Spain was looked up to as a superior power and in 1004 al-Muzaffar was asked to arbitrate in the disputed regency of Christian León. In 1008, at the death of al-Muzaffar, his half-brother Sanchuelo took over. From then on anarchy prevailed, as might be expected with a caliphal nonentity and a feeble "dictator". The details are sad and I avoid them. Factions rose and fell; in 1009 the Berber party obtained the alliance of Castile, whose Count Sancho Garcia sacked Córdoba; in the following year the Berbers took Medina Azzahra as their headquarters, sacked it, burned it and abandoned it. From then on the huge complex was torn apart in a search for base and precious metals, and used as a quarry. Its delicately carved marble column bases and capitals can be seen today in Córdoba, Seville and even Marrakesh, and the fighting bulls that pastured there centuries later were fenced in by shaped stone from the palace of Abderrahman al-Nasir.

The splendid structure that had taken three centuries to build, that had towered over Spain and North Africa, attaining the same eminence as Byzantium, took only twenty-five years to collapse. The Visigothic state, which had lasted as long, fell in even less time. In essence the causes were identical — a self-styled aristocracy, ill-treatment of minorities and failure to remember that a state is composed of subjects, not of rulers. From the ruins of the caliphate emerged about thirty petty states, Arab, Slav and Berber, busier with mutual envy than with the preservation of Islam in the West. But even they, and the dying caliphate before them, were patrons of the arts and allowed a genius such as Ibn Hazm to attain such eminence that he ranks with Seneca, Quevedo and Unamuno, as one of the world's greatest men of letters. The breakdown of the caliphate was ushered in by the dictatorship of Almanzor; unlike that of Charles Martel which set France on the road to greatness, his was but the first step to ruin. But what could exceed the futility of a Caliph whose army "considered that he gave no more evidence of decision than a blind camel", and when he heard the muezzin call to prayer, remarked that it would be more successful to call the Faithful to the pub?

In the final dissolution the Girdle of Zobeida survived unharmed, still flaunting its scorpion clasp flanked by the two great emeralds. One night it passed over the Sierra Morena, escorted by a forest of lances, to shine among the treasures of Ismail al-Tafir, first *taifa*[3] King of Toledo.

Entrance to the walled town of Calatañazor.

CHAPTER FOUR

The Road Back

It seems reasonable that the Spaniards, having lost most of their country to Moslem invaders, should seize the first opportunity of getting it back. Most writers, in fact, accept the claim that refugees in the Cantabrian mountains resolved to drive out the hated pagans and that this was accomplished after eight centuries of glorious warfare. Every Spaniard child is taught that Pelayo was given command of the refugees in a Cantabrian cave and that, at some time between 718 and 725 this remnant of the Visigothic empire inflicted a crushing defeat on an overwhelming force of invaders; the battle was fought at Covadonga, their own missiles recoiled on the Moslems and their Visigothic allies (rarely mentioned), including Archbishop Oppas, and the Reconquest was on. The election of Pelayo is commemorated by a statue and an obelisk in the village below, standing in the field where traditionally he took an oath to restore the Christian monarchy. Even if Pelayo's oath is legend, other evidence supports the existence of the ideal, to restore the Spain of the Visigoths to its old boundaries. But ideals may not always be practicable or, in this case, even desirable. So while chronicles of A.D. 833 already look forward to the end of Saracen domination, they are limited to the kingdom of León; Castile was still to become a separate county and kingdom and later absorb its parent. The Reconquest then became a Castilian dream. Christian nuclei in the Pyrenees, including Navarre and Aragón, wished no more than to keep what they had and to live on good terms with the Moslems, at least until the eleventh century.

Our subject is so bound up with emotion that a candid appraisal is difficult. The Reconquest should be accurately defined, under three headings, in fact: first the recovery of land, implying a sufficiency of labour to make it productive. Secondly, the recovery of wealth, which can be in the form of booty, or of tribute, to be used for further gains. And thirdly, at this time most neglected, the propagation of the Christian faith. History shows that the first and last aspects lagged behind the second. When the caliphate crashed in the first half of the eleventh century it was Castile that was first to profit by the weakness and disunity of the *taifas.* Immediately, then, we meet that side of the Spanish character which has so often denied them the rewards of their heroism and tenacity. The *taifas* were weak because they fought among themselves. The Christian states, when the rest of Spain lay at their feet, behaved in the same way, bickering among each other until a king ruled over two or three, then separating when he bequeathed his kingdom among a number of sons. Not once, but over and over again, they experienced the painful process of union and separation, while Moslem Spain lay at the mercy of a united attack.

It is true that there were not enough Christians to repopulate much conquered territory, but it is too often forgotten that subject Moslems, or *mudéjares*, were just as well behaved as the Mozarabs had been under the emirs and Caliphs. Others point out that the *taifas* paid regular tribute, sometimes to more than one Christian state simultaneously, and in return for protection money were defended against their neighbours. There was trouble when one neighbour had a different protector. Christian kings also took tribute in the form of Moslem troops, so that the former employment of Christian mercenaries by the Caliphs had its counterpart.

It is possible, too, that Christian and Moslem realised their basic kinship and there is no doubt that the former appreciated the artistic and industrial skill of the latter. Foreign knights, imbued with the spirit of crusading, could not understand the generous terms granted to defeated Moslems; far from being expelled from every newly won acre, they were usually allowed to keep their goods, their towns and their fields. Thus was continued an old Spanish custom. The Moslems began it by permitting Christians to remain for the taxes they paid and, in the early days, for the crafts they could teach. Now the Christians were establishing protectorates of conquered Moslems because they had no wish to depopulate their new territories and ruin their trade and agriculture. As Enrique Sordo says of a later stage of the Reconquest, "the truth is that the whole of Christian Spain had lived for centuries off the taxes paid by the Moors". But the majority of our writers, when they stray from the beaten path of *corrida, fiesta* and *flamenco*, still reveal in the phrase, ". . . groaning for centuries under the Moorish yoke".

Denigrating the enemy is of course a recognised form of warfare. Divine support works even better and has also been employed for as long as written records exist. The Spanish were therefore greatly heartened, not only by the discovery of St James the Greater's remains in the ninth century, but by the flow of pilgrims that made their way, mostly through Christian territory, to his last resting place, Santiago de Compostela. The reigning King of Asturias, Alfonso II, took a leading part in honouring the sacred relics. Santiago (St James) himself was credited with appearing in person at the Battle of Clavijo in 845, fought to rid the Christians of the annual tribute of a hundred maidens. The Saint's contribution to victory was the personal slaying of 60,000 "Moors", whence his title *"Matamoros"* and the numerous representations of the miracle in churches and museums. Although it is now admitted that there was no tribute of maidens and no Battle of Clavijo, the story was good enough to keep up the fighting spirit of the northeners, if that were ever necessary. It persisted at least into the sixteenth century, when the patron was clearly seen by Cortés' men in a battle against Mexicans. And it travelled far afield, for it is said that when Shah Abbas the Great of Persia (1587 – 1629) was about to make an especially fierce shot at polo he would invoke Santiago, whom the Persians identified with Mohamed's son-in-law, Ali.

Santiago's fame indeed was such that the pilgrimage became the most important in Western Europe, ranking immediately after Jerusalem and Rome, and attracting, among other famous votaries, Chaucer's Wife of Bath. In addition, Santiago was a shareholder in the financial department of the Reconquest. From the ninth century he was entitled to his portion of corn or wine from every acre of ploughed land or vineyard and at the division of booty he received the share allotted to a knight, a bigger income than would appear at first sight, as he could hardly avoid being present at every successful engagement, or being absent at others.

But Santiago served Spain more effectively than as a mere warrior. Around the year 1000 new trends arose in the relations of the Christian kingdoms; Castile and Aragón, later to unify and control the whole of Spain, take the stage for the first time, while Navarre, under Sancho the Great, emerges for only a moment as a significant power. Where the chief pilgrims' road crossed the Pyrenees Sancho's mountain kingdom absorbed the cultural and political spirit of France, later passing it on to Castile. So it was the pilgrims who really opened Christian Spain to the outside world; because of them Sancho invited the Benedictine monks of Cluny, foremost in culture at that time, to bring their education and handicrafts and settle. They smoothed the pilgrims' way with roads and bridges, a number of which are still in use.

Think for a moment what this meant. From the Romans through the Visigoths, under whom Isidore flourished, to the Caliphate and the *taifas*, there was no break in the chain of culture. And now, even while the moribund *taifas* were vying with each other in fostering science and the arts, a new culture was coming in from the north, a culture that, for all its rawness, was linked to the more spiritual ideals of Christianity. During the centuries that passed while the rest of Europe was painfully struggling towards the light, only Spain and Sicily knew no Dark Ages.

Politically too, their arrival was of importance, for Cluny produced Pope Gregory VII, the great Hildebrand. Even during the reign of Alexander II his predecessor, reports from Cluny began to reach Rome and led the Pope in 1063 to classify the Reconquest as a crusade, a generation before the first crusade to the Holy Land. From now on Christian Spain lay open to anyone of "blood and coat armour" who saw before him the rewards of both piety and avarice. As in the better known Eastern crusades the younger son was tempted by the prospect of using his sword to slay the infidel and thus carve for himself a fief, or feudal territory. The glittering prospect was stressed by the Spanish kings, in a recruiting campaign, hinting optimistically at the rich rewards awaiting the brave knight; hence the couplet in the fourteenth century "Romaunt of the Rose",[1]

"Though shalt make castels than in Spayne,
And dreme of joy, al but in vayne."

As the *taifas* became weaker the Moslems became not only tolerant but positively respectful. When King Ferdinand,I was raiding the lands of Seville and the emir proposed to buy him off, the price demanded was the body of the martyred Saint Justa. A deputation of bishops duly arrived in Seville, to be told that no one could find the martyr's bones; before they could return, however, to report a fruitless mission the body of Saint Isidore was miraculously revealed to them. What followed has been recorded in lively fashion in a Latin chronicle: how the Emir Benehabet (Mu'tadid Ibn Abbad), unbeliever though he was, feared the power of the Lord; how he asked them, "If I give you Isidore what have I left?" and how eventually, when the party was leaving, "Behold the King of the Saracens, the above-named Benehabet, threw a beautifully embroidered drape over the casket and emitting great sighs from deep in his bosom said 'Ah, how far you are going from here, O Isidore worshipful man! But you yourself know how your cause is mine too' ". The old hypocrite. He reconciled his piety with the habit of keeping his enemies' skulls in jewelled caskets and gloating over them from time to time.

ALFONSO VI. When Ferdinand I died in 1065 he left the usual muddle. His territories were divided among his sons: Sancho, the eldest, got Castile; Alfonso, the second, inherited León, which ranked higher; and Galicia went to the third son, Garcia. As usual, fighting began as soon as the funeral was over. Each son had inherited the right to collect protection money from one or more of the *taifas* and greed led to squabbles; in one of these the Cid, destined to become more famous than his masters, earned the enmity of rival protectors. To settle the rivalry between León and Castile the elder brothers decided, at a friendly meeting, that the result of a battle should be taken as the will of God, and that the winner should take all.

The battle was fought at Llantada in July 1068. Alfonso lost. But there was no handing over of León; a poor sportsman, he held on to his patrimony and was lucky enough to have the support of one of his *taifa* kings, Mamun Ibn Di-l-Nun of Toledo. You may remember him as the father of St Casilda. Later, when the Moslem king of Badajoz was dying, Alfonso attacked his *taifa*; with Mamun as mediator the men of León agreed to retire in exchange for an annual tribute, in addition to the one being paid to García of Galicia. After the king of Badajoz died his two sons quarrelled and Alfonso again stepped in to demand an increase in the agreed tribute; when this was refused he raised an army to attack and plunder.

A while later Sancho and Alfonso, the two strong brothers, shelved their quarrel and decided what to do about the third, García of Galicia. García took refuge with his *taifa* client of Seville and his brothers amicably divided Galicia. Later Alfonso offered García a friendly invitation to talk things over; having accepted, he arrived, was put in chains and imprisoned in the castle of Luna, near León. After seventeen years the prisoner showed signs of dying so the tender-hearted Alfonso ordered his chains to be struck off. The obstinate prisoner refused, preferring to be buried in the fetters he had worn so long. Meanwhile Alfonso had enjoyed the income of García's *taifas*; it possibly promoted the Reconquest which, you will agree, differed markedly from the knightly ideals of a crusade and from the accounts usually given in history books.

But in 1072, five years after the indecisive battle of Llantada, Sancho once more attacked his brother and again defeated him, this time at Golpejera. Generously he allowed Alfonso to take refuge with his client Mamun; historians report that he used the nine months of Mamun's hospitality to spy out Toledo's weak points — an obvious invention as Toledo was won without an assulat or pitched battle. Sancho meanwhile attacked Zamora, the property of his sister; his commander, *alférez*, or ensign, was the Cid, whose fantastic career touches this story only occasionally. There the King of Castile was killed by a bold stroke, usually called treachery, although it is one of the few honourable episodes of the age. The *Portillo de la Traición*, through which the assassin is said to have regained the shelter of the city, can still be seen.

Alfonso was now able to return from exile and in order to assume the combined crowns of León and Castile (which had been Sancho's) he had to take the famous oath disclaiming responsibility for his brother's murder. The custom conformed partly with Visigothic law, partly with Roman. The king was supported by twelve men of standing – again we meet the "twelve good men and true" – placed his hands on the Gospel and on an iron lock on the altar and swore three times that he had no hand in Sancho's murder. The customary oath was administered by the military chief, in this case the Cid; who, on completing the ceremony, tried to kiss the monarch's hand, Alfonso refused to allow him to do so. Hence because of his pallor and suspicious bearing, arose the story that he had a guilty conscience.

The facts are that Alfonso was a domineering ruler and the Cid a successful warrior; intolerant to his inferiors, Alfonso was also prejudiced against his betters. The following well-known episode gives an insight into his character. In 1074 he had married the first

The statue of Pelayo, the legendary pioneer of the Reconquest. (*Lee Weatherley*)

of his four or five wives, Inés, daughter of the powerful Duke of Aquitaine. Possibly due to her influence there was a move against the retention of the mozarabic liturgy, at that time dear to all Spanish Christians, to whom it represented centuries of a faith upheld in the heart of Islam. Conformity with the rest of the Catholic world was urged by wife, pope and the monks of Cluny. The argument became heated when Pope Gregory VII depreciated the work of St Isidore and other venerated Spanish clerics, classing the Goths (from whom the aristocracy proudly claimed descent) with the Moors. A decisive trial of arms was decreed at Burgos in 1077; the champion for the Mozarabic rite was a Castilian, Lope Martinez, and his opponent, strangely enough, a Mozarab from Toledo. When Martinez won the Catholic party was dissatisfied and another trial, this time by fire, was ordered. Both liturgies were thrown into the bonfire but, miraculously, the Mozarabic one sprang out of the flames. Never a man to be thwarted, Alfonso kicked it back, with the oft-quoted remark,

> "*Allá van leyes* (Laws go the way kings want)
> *Do quieren reyes.*"

Cluny thus triumphed and a few years later even the Toledan or Visigothic script was superseded by the French.

In the year after the trial the newly widowed Alfonso married Constance of Burgundy; the wedding service was conducted by her neighbour, the Abbott of Cluny, and all went merrily, especially for Alfonso, who spent most of the honeymoon with the bridesmaid. Since the beginning of the tenth century the kings of León had styled themselves "Emperor"; it is only coincidence that another and more famous emperor, Frederick II Hohenstaufen, imitated Alfonso's nuptial flight when he married Yolande, heiress to Jerusalem, over a century later.

In the same year Alfonso, now feeling secure in his own possessions, began the offensive against the *taifas*. His host Mamun had died, leaving a grandson Alcádir to reign in Toledo. The key to the control of the Tagus was Coria, and Alfonso won its castle without difficulty. Strictly speaking, it was in the *taifa* of Badajoz, but the man who kicked a liturgy into the fire was not the man to worry about kicking Moslem ambassadors when they came to protest. At about this time occurred an episode which, even if legendary, surely gives us an insight into the Emperor's mentality. He marched his army towards Seville, which was too weak to oppose it. The vizier Ibn Amar, as slippery as Alfonso and even more cunning. came to visit the Christian camp as an envoy; he brought with him a marvellously decorated set of chessmen and a board of ebony and ivory. Alfonso, as you might expect, fancied himself as a player; the upshot was a challenge, and Alfonso was to have the chess set if he won. And if he lost? Well, Ibn Amar hardly thought this would happen, and flattering courtiers agreed that the question was purely academic; Ibn Amar shrugged and said that in that case he would ask for some favour or other. Alfonso lost. This time there was no ignoring the conditions, as after the Battle of Llantada or at the bonfire of Burgos. He cursed and he growled,

(above) Alfonso VI from the Cathedral at Santiago.

(left) Alfonso II (called "the chaste"), who is largely responsible for launching the cult of Santiago.

(below) A sixteenth-century representation of the Cid.

but his courtiers had heard the terms of the match and could not advise evading them. Ibn Amar had blandly asked that Alfonso take his army back home; white with rage, he was persuaded that it had to be done, in view of the public wager. The story is commemorated in a mediaeval fresco in the Cathedral of Le Puy in France, a reminder of the ease with which stories, as well as pilgrims, went back and forth between Christian Europe and al-Andalus.

In 1085 Toledo fell, as a result of secret negotiations. A "face-saving" siege lasted four years and the hungry defenders, when the supply of flour gave out, made do with a paste of sugar and ground almonds – *mazapan*, whence marzipan – an early version of "Let them eat cake". Now Alfonso called himself "*Imperator totius Hispaniae*" but events and his own haughtiness would soon belie the claim. Far from being Emperor of all Spain, he would have difficulty in preserving his own heritage and Toledo. But its capture ranked as the most important single event of the century in Spain, and the whole of Christian Europe rejoiced. By the terms of surrender Alcádir was to leave his property intact and was allowed to keep the city of Valencia as compensation. No one knew that a company of poor merchants had left for Cuenca a few days earlier carrying a fortune in jewels in their panniers and that one of them had the Girdle of Zobeida clasped round his middle, under his ragged tunic. And so it remained Alcádir's, to continue its adventures in Valencia.

The Portillo de la Traición at Zamora.

CHAPTER FIVE

The Men from Morocco

In the meantime a huge new empire had arisen in North Africa. The ancestors of the modern Touareg, the Sanhadja, were camel breeders who wandered over the Sahara. Some of them settled on the Upper Niger and combined their tastes for blood and mysticism by founding communities of fighting monks, the *al-Murabitun* or (as the Spaniards pronounced it) Almoravids. The name comes from the Arabic *ribat*, roughly meaning a monastery, and the next fifty years saw the fighting monks build an empire that extended from Ghana to Morocco and Algeria.

When Alfonso used his capture of Toledo, not to further the reconquest of territory but to extort more money from the *taifas*, there was muttering among the Spanish Moslems and thoughts turned to the new empire across the straits. When he became positively tyrannical a cry for help came from the Moslem King of Seville to old Yusuf Ibn Tasufin emir of the Almoravids. As *imam* he was entitled not only to conduct public worship but to declare the *jehad*, or holy war. This he did, and was soon marching from Algeciras at the head of his desert warriors (forerunners of the Templars and other religious orders) and with little trouble defeated Alfonso and his confederate army of Leonese, Castilians, Aragonese, French and Italians at the battle of Sagrajas (1086). It was typical of Yusuf and the North African invaders generally that they never hesitated to sacrifice their Spanish Moslem allies, whom they regarded as renegades; but after these had sustained the first shock of battle they charged into the mêlée with their disciplined horde of negroes, war drums beating and spears clashing against shields of hippopotamus hide.

Yusuf, though he despised the *taifa* kings, kept his word and went back to Morocco. But the Spanish Moslems could not resist the remorseless pressure of the Christians and in 1090 they had to ask Yusuf to come and help them again. This time the Almoravids came to stay, inflicting defeat after defeat on the Christians while they appropiated the *taifas*. From now on we are correct in speaking of a "Moorish" domination in Spain. I have discussed the name "Moor"; it is best left alone until the advent of the Almoravids. They sustained only one defeat, before Valencia at the hands of the Cid. The free lance hero had captured the city in 1094 after the unfortunate Alcádir had been hunted down and killed by fellow Moslems, who found the Girdle of Zobeida concealed beneath his clothes. The *cadi*, leader of the revolution-aries, kept the girdle and later swore that he had never seen it. Under torture he confessed that it was hidden where even today the Arab hides his valuables, in the *takh al-ballat* under the floor of the harem. So once more the girdle, sinister now with the blood that had been shed for it, changed hands. It is said that Jimena, the Cid's wife, would never wear it and it accompanied the dead hero to Castile in 1102, when Valencia had to be abandoned to the Almoravids. By the Cid's will the kings of Castile inherited it. While the Cid was capturing and holding Valencia the Almoravids had been successful elsewhere, mastering everything except civil-isation. They say that a poet recited his most famous verses before the Moorish emir Yusuf; asked his opinion of them, the savage conqueror replied, "I only know that he wants money."

Meanwhile Alfonso had re-married several times in the hope of fathering a male heir, who persistently eluded him. In 1091, however, Mu'tamid of Seville (son of the old scoundrel who handed over the body of St Isidore) encouraged his widowed daughter-in-law Zaida to become Alfonso's concubine. Though some authors feel the relationship to be below the dignity of a *reconquistador* there is little doubt that he was not free to marry her, though she changed her religion and was baptised Isabel. She soon produced the desired son, but the lad was killed in the last of Alfonso's many defeats by the Almoravids, the disastrous battle of Uclés. Alfonso died the next year, on 30th June, 1109. Though esteemed chiefly as a hero of the Reconquest and the conqueror of Toledo, his most important work for Spain was the road to Santiago and the forging of cultural links with France.

Under the Almoravids intolerance and persecution appeared for the first time in al-Andalus, little distinction being made between Arabs, Mozarabs and Jews. In vain did the *taifa* kings now seek alliance with Castile; one by one they were deposed and at last Moslem Spain was again united. But not for long. Internal dissension produced a second crop of *taifas*, which weakened Almoravid authority in Africa and finally overwhelmed them.

A new sect of fanatics, the mountaineer Almohads or unitarians, arose. Reacting against the rigid control and extortion practised by the Almoravids, they became a conquering faction; they displaced the Almoravids after a fifty years' rule in Spain, which continued to be governed by ignorant, uncivilised and fanatical foreigners, whose headquarters and spiritual home were in Morocco. Again we hear of a Caliph (the Almohads were ambitious) listening to a poet and not understanding his verses: "Sit down, you bore me", he is said to have ordered. Internecine strife was repeated and in 1212 the decisive battle of Las Navas de Tolosa was won by the rare combination of Castile, León, Navarre and Aragón, with considerable help from such allies as the Knights Templar.

That was the end of any serious threat from Africa, though the next Moroccan dynasty, the Marinids, dabbled unsuccessfully in Spanish politics. After Las Navas de Tolosa the Reconquest really got under way; Ferdinand III of Castile – later St Ferdinand – united Castile and León and reconquered Jaén, Córdoba and Seville. In marked contrast to the fanatics from Morocco, most of the Christian kings were tolerant of other religions, to the benefit of their country; some, beginning with Alfonso VI, even styled themselves "Emperor of the two (or three) religions".

The Almoravids left no tangible record of their rule in Spain except their name for the common *dinar*, a coin called *maravedi* which circulated as late as the nineteenth century. The Almohads, on the other hand, were builders and, though they may have relied to a great extent on the craftsmen of subject peoples, at least left such treasures as the Giralda in Seville and the Tower of Gold in the same city. We shall see that Spanish architecture and decoration owe much to Arabic influence, chiefly through subject *mudéjares*, but partly through the fused Visigothic and Islamic style of emigrated Mozarabs. By driving them and the Jews from al-Andalus the Moors did Christian Spain a great service.

The Kingdom of Granada arose through the shrewdness of an Arab when St Ferdinand was conquering huge tracts of the south; it survived because of the prevailing climate of the Reconquest, more interested in money (protection money amounted to 150,000 *maravedies* a year) than religion, or even land. The Arab was named Ibn al-Ahmar ("Son of the red man") and he offered allegiance to the Christian king; Ferdinand accepted and a treaty was duly signed. Later, in accordance with its terms, Ibn al-Ahmar had to assist St Ferdinand at the siege of his co-religionists in Seville. After its successful conclusion he returned to Granada, sad and humiliated, to find triumphal arches and cheering throngs of Moslems hailing him as "El Ghalib", the Conqueror, not a whit disturbed by the fact that it was their fellow Moslems who had been conquered for the benefit of the Christian unbelievers. "*Wala ghalib ill'Allah*" (There is no conqueror but Allah) said the unhappy hero. The sentence was inscribed on a "bend" of his coat-of-arms, adopted as the family motto, and can now be seen as one of the chief decorations in the Alhambra[1], and also in the family crest of a descendant who had been converted to Christianity.

ALFONSO X. Son of the great St Ferdinand, he was his father's opposite in every quality. Where the latter had been a great soldier, a wise administrator and a devoted husband, Alfonso was woefully deficient in each activity. But he more than made up for his shortcomings by his brilliance as a scholar and his patronage of the arts, sciences and literature. His Spanish grandmother had much to do with his education, an advanced one for those days; his descent, in the proportion of less than two parts Spanish to one Greek and one Franco-German, possibly accounted for his enquiring mind and originality. He would probably have been proficient enough in traditional pursuits; he was distinguished as a soldier and *reconquistador* – but only in his youth. He fought against the Marinids of Morocco. With Moslem Granada as his ally he took Jerez, Arcos de la Frontera, Lebrija and Medina Sidonia; without its help he reconquered Lorca and Cartagena. Later, still in customary fashion, he turned on his Granadine allies and

The statue of Maimonides near
his house in Córdoba.

defeated them to the tune of an annual tribute of 250,000 marks.

His family was already renowned throughout Europe and in 1254 he gave the accolade of knighthood to a distinguished visitor. Edward, Earl of Chester and future Edward I of England, had come to be affianced to Eleanor of Castile and the honour was bestowed in the royal convent of Las Huelgas, near Burgos. In 1262, ten years after his coronation, Alfonso had his last triumphs: the Castilian fleet captured Cádiz and he prevented the great James I of Aragón, his father-in-law, from keeping the recently conquered Province of Murcia. Thereafter he seems to have lost interest in warfare.

He brought the same negligence to the task of ruling. Through his mother, Beatrice of Swabia, he had a good claim to the title of Holy Roman Emperor; to further this ambition he had to pacify the greedy nobles of León and Castile, thus plunging the country into a financial crisis. In contesting the election with Richard of Cornwall and, later, Rudolf of Hapsburg, he spent another ten million escudos[2]; cardinals and German electors were openly bribed in those and later days. Though elected he was later forced to relinquish his claim. To remedy his extravagance he could think of no better solutions than to debase the coinage and pawn his crown with the King of Morocco, from whom he also obtained military aid. Later he tried the expedient of arresting rich Jews and releasing them against a payment. As most of his intellectual

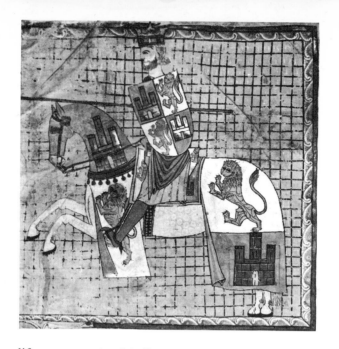

Alfonso X (called "the Learned").

life was spent with Jews, and he had presented them with three mosques in Seville for use as synagogues, we can assume that he was desperately hard up.

Like all irresolute men, he tried to atone for his weakness by occasional exhibitions of petulance, which he confused with firmness. His first act, on coming to the throne, was to send away and threaten to divorce his wife Violante (Yolande), daughter of the powerful King of Aragón, James I known as el Conquistador. His excuse was her sterility and it is typical of Alfonso that he forgot to verify this: in the event she was pregnant and bore him three children in all. The elder son died after producing heirs; while these were still infants Alfonso's second son Sancho claimed the succession. Alfonso, always the pedant, insisted on his grandchildren inheriting, in accordance with his own unpopular code of laws. The nobles and most of the towns backed Sancho; only Seville remained faithful, for which she was rewarded with the rebus that still figures in her crest: "No 8 Do". The figure in the middle, like an elongated "8", is a skein or *madeja*, so that the puzzle reads: "No madeja Do", or "No m'ha dejado" — "She has not abandoned me."

His final stupidity was to advertise his lack of piety; here he might have taken a lesson from Almanzor. Like many intellectuals, he was regarded with suspicion and when it became known that he had remarked about the Creation, "If the Almighty had consulted me, I could have suggested some improvements", his rebellious subjects had just the weapon they needed. It is only fair to add that the remark was first recorded a century later, in the Chronicle of Pedra IV of Aragón, an enemy of the royal house of Castile. If it was made, the boast was uttered in Alfonso's observatory, in the Castle of Segovia (colour plate) which was struck by lightning next day; like his subjects, Alfonso regarded this as cause and effect and became pious again, donning the rope girdle of the Franciscans. Too late, alas. The Cortes, or Parliament, met in Valladolid in 1282 and deposed him. When he died two years later even his will was ignored.

You may wonder why I have devoted so much space to so futile a character, and how he got his nickname "El Sabio". In this case the word means, not "Wise", but "Learned". Indeed, he was so famous as a scholar that the Sultan of Cairo sent him a strange collection of presents with the request that Alfonso send a daughter to grace his harem. The giraffe aroused great interest; the zebra was given to Sancho, who sent it to the Marinid emir in Morocco; the stuffed crocodile was hung in the Orange Patio of Seville Cathedral, and you can still see the excellent wooden replica that was substituted when it fell to pieces.

One of Alfonso's improvements was the use of the Castilian and Galician tongues in place of Latin. His school of translators at Toledo, descended from that of the *taifa*, employed Jews who knew both Arabic and Castilian; through them even translations from Sanskrit were achieved. In refusing to have the translations in Latin he imitated his cousin, the Emperor Frederick of Sicily, who was responsible for the adoption of the vernacular in Italy. And, in the same way as the latter encouraged the composition of poetry in Italian, so Alfonso produced the poetic canticles (*cantigas*) in honour of the Blessed Virgin, in Galician. It is believed that these were an inspiration to the troubadours. Jurisprudence was another of his interests and his *Siete Partidas*, which was to cause the trouble with Sancho, was a blend of Visigothic-Roman law and Justinian's *Institutes*. Well ahead of its time, it was adopted in Castile in the next century and throughout Spain in 1492.

It has been said that the spirit of the thirteenth century created four significant innovations: Gothic architecture, the *Summa Theologiae* of St Thomas Aquinas, the *Divina Commedia* of Dante and the *Partidas* of Alfonso. The claim has an additional meaning

Mosaic tiles at the
Alhambra in Granada.

for us when we remember that Dante's work was based on the account of Mohamed's night flight, made available to western Europe in the Toledo translation, *La Escala de Mahoma*. Apart from the foregoing, Alfonso and his Arabs and Jews were responsible for advances in astronomy; his tables took Toledo as the meridian and were used three centuries later by Copernicus. His contribution to history, as well as his encouragement of research in music, was also of great importance, but with so much to his credit it is impossible to dwell on any but his most outstanding works. It is worth noting, nevertheless, that he could write books on hunting and indoor games, with a section on chess. Such a man cannot be dismissed as a mere bungler.

Nothing happens in an intellectual vacuum and Alfonso's work was indebted to his predecessors. When Alfonso VI took Toledo two centuries earlier he found a huge library and a wealth of Arab and Jewish talent. Under the archbishops a flourishing trilingual school arose and welcomed the distinguished visitors whom I named in Chapter 3; they all translated Arabic versions of ancient Greek works via Romance into Latin. Michael Scot was another who had used his time in Toledo to translate mathematical treatises and works of Aristotle before going to the equally fruitful centre of Palermo. Even St Thomas Aquinas, mentioned above as one of the century's innovators, owed much to the Spanish Moslem Averroes and the Cordoban Jew Maimonides.

The process is well exemplified by Hermanus Alemannus (Herman the German) of Toledo, who began by translating Aristotle and Averroes into Latin and proceeded, under Alfonso X, to render the Book of Psalms in Castilian. Other

Germans, forerunners of Dr Faustus, flocked to Toledo with the avowed intention of learning the black arts, for in the twelfth century a Toledo magician had sent a coven of witches to Conrad of Marburg. The reader, brought up in the belief that Spain has always been the home of bigotry, may be excused his surprise. It has been stated often, but realised rarely, that Spain was in advance of the rest of Europe in learning and liberality. Salamanca and Alcalá had women professors who, though after Novella d'Andrea of Bologna, were the successors of feminine Moslem lecturers. The Christian kingdoms assured the privileges of the nobility long before our Magna Carta, and Spanish burghers anticipated by many years our claim to have founded the Mother of Parliaments.

With all his ineptitude, Alfonso *el Sabio* deserved well of Spain – better, perhaps, than historians have acknowledged. He lost money, lands and even his crown (apart from pawning it, that is). None of his ambitions was fulfilled and he died a lonely man, conscious only of failure. And yet he played a greater part in the advancement of the human spirit than did all the practitioners of blood and plunder, both before and after. Let us not compare him with the heroes of the Reconquest, nor with the empire builders; rather let us see him as fellow to his cousin, Frederick Hohenstaufen, or as an Erasmus forever stumbling over the trappings of royalty.

The Torre del Oro in Seville.

The Ruins of the Castillo de Alcalá de Guadiara (a Moorish castle near Seville).

CHAPTER SIX

The Trastámaras

The marriage between Alfonso *el Sabio* and the daughter of James I of Aragón, conqueror of Valencia and the Balearic Islands, was only one link between Castile and Aragón. In fact four such marriages took place between 1128 and 1249. You might think, therefore, that harmony prevailed among the Christian states. You would be wrong. The intrepid Spaniard is fiercely independent and talk of union has usually been feared as much as heresy. The countries had a totally different outlook: Castile looked south to reconquest and the occupation of North Africa; Aragón to the east, where Sicily and Athens were but two possessions of James I's descendants. The capture of Valencia represented, for them, additional Mediterranean bases for trade and conquest, rather than a step forward in a holy war. This chapter deals mainly with Castile and much of it teems with human interest. But from now on, for over two centuries, intermittent war between and in the Christian kingdoms slows down the Reconquest, as does the disloyalty of greedy, revolting (in both senses) nobles.

PEDRO THE CRUEL. I wish I could explain why Peter the Cruel is nearly always called Pedro in English books, while Enrique of Trastámara is called Henry and Henry the Impotent is called Enrique; it matters little, so long as the reader knows that the choice of names is haphazard.

Was Pedro cruel? Or did he rather deserve his other title, *el Justiciero*, the Just? The anecdotes left by his partisans and

Pedro I ("the Cruel")
of Castile.

enemies are so conflicting that we shall probably never be able to make a fair assessment of his character, but it is noteworthy that Isabel the Catholic and Philip II (both tending to be bigoted) rehabilitated his memory. The events of his reign largely hinge on the fact that his father Alfonso XI had ten illegitimate children surnamed de las Mercedes; of whom the eldest, the twins Henry and Fadrique, were older than the legitimate Pedro. Now Pedro was alleged to have conspired in the murder of their mother, Leonor de Guzmán, and of his own wife, the French Blanche of Bourbon, whom he had abandoned after two days of marriage. Many accept the story that Pedro's half-brother Fadrique, Master of Santiago, was sent to fetch Blanche from France, that their journey to Spain included a trip to Cythera, and that the result of their indiscretion was a boy called Enriquez, who was brought up in Seville by a nurse known as La Paloma (the Dove) and who eventually fathered a line holding the hereditary office of Admirals of Castile. Though the office itself was something of a sinecure the Castilian navy was a power to be respected in the Bay of Biscay, where it was a perpetual threat to England's communications with her territories of Poitou and Gascony. The Hundred Years' War between England and France, incidentally, is the pivot round which the alliances of Pedro and his enemies turn.

Whether the scandal involving Blanche was true or false, the children of Leonor de Guzmán had further reason to hate Pedro when he had Fadrique clubbed to death in the Alcázar of Seville. Another tale concerns his treatment of "Mohamed the Red" of Granada. This usurper of the throne was evicted and came for refuge to Pedro without a safe conduct. Pedro, however, was an ally of the rightful king of Granada, now safely back on his throne. This gave him sufficient excuse to murder Mohamed the Red and steal (or as we say today, nationalise) his jewels, among them a great ruby which, like Zobeida's girdle, keeps cropping up in history.

The Alcázar, still one of the show places of Seville, was originally the Moorish citadel, but what one sees today is almost solely the work of builders employed by Pedro in 1364. This is recorded in the Lombardic lettering of the main facade where, almost inevitably, the Moorish craftsmen sent by his friend the rightful king of Granada added eight times, in Arabic script, "There is no conqueror but Allah". For all its over-elaboration and ill-advised attempts at restoration by later kings the Alcázar still gives the visitor, if he is not too exacting, the feeling of wandering through a Moorish palace. (Note for instance, the resemblance between the Alcázar of Seville and a patio in the Nasrid palace of the Alhambra.) Here is a repository of *mudéjar*, if not Moorish, art. On every side are geometric designs, repeated in the *artesonado* ceilings with their inlay of painted wood and ivory, as well as intricately patterned wall tiles, or *azulejos*, and pierced windows of stone and stucco, the so-called *Qamariyyah* or *Shamshiyya*. Every room has its history and even the tiles of the staircase walls carry the *Plus Ultra* motto of Charles V. Pedro the Cruel's bedroom shows four painted skulls over the door commemorating, so it is said, unjust judges whom he had executed. In this wealth of display it is worth spending a few extra minutes in the gorgeous Hall of the Ambassadors, usually, and incorrectly, pointed out as the site of Fadrique's murder.

Pedro had a beautiful mistress, Maria de Padilla, and claimed that they were married; even today her coffin, which lies next to his in Seville Cathedral, describes her as his wife. If she was, then their daughters were rightful heirs to the throne of Castile, which would therefore have passed to John of Gaunt, who married the elder. But this second half of the fourteenth century in Spain was a period of reaction against legitimacy. Pedro's end, in fact, could be termed (for lovers of the sensational) "The Day of the Bastards".

Several anecdotes support his title of "the Just". One of them was told to a traveller in the eighteenth century: an irascible canon of Seville Cathedral, dissatisfied with a pair of shoes, beat the unfortunate shoemaker to death with his own last. The widow and her five children, the eldest a boy of fourteen, brought the matter to court and the canon was sentenced to a year's exclusion from the chapter. The boy grew up, followed his father's trade and somehow managed to provide for the family. One day, watching the famous Holy Week procession, his rage got the better of him; he hurled himself at the canon and stabbed him to death. His trial was a summary one and he was sentenced to be hanged, drawn and quartered. Pedro, "whom we call the Cruel", says Peyron, "but whom the Spanish more rightly call the Just",[1] himself constituted a court of appeal and confirmed the verdict but altered the sentence; the revised punishment was that the young murderer was prohibited from carrying on his trade as a shoemaker *for a period of one year.*

Pedro became unpopular with the nobles on two main counts: first, because he had liberal ideas and tended to support his plebeian subjects rather than the *ricos hombres* and *hijosdalgo* who, exempt from taxation, were a useless and even mischievous burden in peacetime. Secondly, Pedro professed great affection for the Jews, who not only provided him with the funds he needed for war against the Moors when he recaptured Elche, but also helped him with money and arms against his half-brothers. We have seen evidence of this, too, in one of the synagogues of Toledo. His extraordinary toleration of the hated race seems to have annoyed Henry almost as much as the murder of his mother and twin brother for, in a conversation with du Guesclin reported by Froissart, he refers to Pedro as "this Jew".

The pattern has by now become familiar enough; progress versus reaction, with nations backing one or other side according to their political, and not their ideological, promptings. The prolonged struggle between Pedro and his half-brother Henry de las Mercedes, Count of Trastámara, should therefore be regarded in this way; more frequently it is explained as a revolt of decency against the excesses of the monarch. But whatever the motives may have been, events moved as follows: from 1335 Henry made repeated attempts to usurp the throne. For a time he sought refuge in Aragón, whose aid he enlisted, and then in France. In both cases his hosts' interests were served by supporting Henry. The French king, for instance, still smarting under the defeats of Crecy, Auray and Poitiers, now saw how the Spanish conflict might help him against England, who counted Pedro as an ally. If Henry gained the throne with France's support the Castilian navy would be a powerful offensive weapon[2]; in addition, he could find useful foreign employment for the free or "white" companies who infested France. In this he had the support of the Pope who had virtually been held to ransom by them in Avignon.

So Bertrand du Guesclin, ransomed for the purpose from Sir John Chandos who had taken him prisoner at Auray, came with the free companies and put Pedro to flight; he was rewarded with a dukedom and for the first time French titles of rank were introduced into Spain. Perhaps the importance of the unedifying squabble lay in the generosity with which Henry rewarded the nobles making them more powerful and independent but exhausting the royal treasury. Castile was to suffer for hundreds of years from this misplaced benevolence – or was it weakness? It was the old story of the decline of feudalism again. "From a protector", says Davis,[3] "the petty lord had degenerated into a pest of society" and his castles "were centres of rebellion and indiscriminate rapine". It is not surprising that later kings had to introduce and revive ordinances against private ownership of certain fortresses.

Pedro meanwhile sought refuge with the Black Prince, whose court was at Bordeaux. A motley force, among whom such seasoned warriors as Chandos and Manny held commands, crossed the Pyrenees with Pedro in search of honour and wealth, and to ensure that the navy of Castile should remain in friendly hands. The decisive battle was fought near Navarrete, on the pilgrims' road that had been so well cared for by Alfonso VI. In this flat, uninteresting country nothing remains to mark the site of the

Black Prince's third great victory. Du Guesclin was captured again and released almost immediately; the Spanish captives were not so lucky, but at least had the Black Prince's chivalry (or his need of ransoms) to thank for their lives. Then came the reckoning, in its literal sense. The Black Prince presented his bill for money advanced and services rendered. Pedro found his treasury in Seville empty, his Italian admiral having absconded with the contents. He gave what he could – some jewellery, notably the huge ruby of the Red King of Granada. This was later worn by Henry V at Agincourt, probably in the gold crown studded with pearls, rubies and sapphires that encircled his gold-plated helmet, dented in the battle and now standing over the king's grave in Westminster Abbey. It was also worn by Richard III at Bosworth Field, and was presumably in the crown which Stanley presented to Richmond, saying:

"Lo! here, this long usurped royalty
From the dead temples of this bloody wretch
Have I pluck'd off, to grace thy brows withal."[4]

It is still to be seen in the Crown of State, worn by each new Sovereign after the coronation ceremony.

However, a few jewels were no substitute for the hard cash that had been spent, and was still owing. The Black Prince waited through the summer, while his men were reduced by dysentery and desertion, until in the late autumn he led back a fifth of the splendid army which had passed through Roncesvalles.[5] The retirement of the English was just what Henry was waiting for; with du Guesclin once more at his side he raised a fresh army and besieged Toledo. When Pedro marched to its relief the rivals met at Montiel, in whose castle Pedro took refuge after the defeat of his army. An eyewitness completes the story. Taking a leaf out of Scipio's book, Henry surrounded Montiel with a stone wall. Du Guesclin was then approached by one of the besieged with a bribe of townships and 200,000 gold doubloons if he would allow Pedro to escape. This du Guesclin's knightly honour and loyalty to the King of France would not permit, but the code of chivalry allowed him to *pretend* to accept Pedro's offer. So Pedro and a few of his followers arrived one night in du Guesclin's tent in their riding clothes; here they were detained by various excuses until Henry

Alvaro de Luna painted by Sancho de Samora, Juan de Segovia and Pedro de Guerniel.

appeared in full armour, helmet and all, and had Pedro pointed out to him by one du Guesclin's knights, "for it was a long time that he had not seen him". Hurling himself at his brother, Henry wounded him in the face; desperately the unarmed Pedro grappled with him until they fell to the ground locked in each other's arms; there the rival kings fought like snarling dogs among the rushes. Pedro, being the stronger, was soon on top, but du Guesclin took him by the foot and pulled him off; then Henry's dagger, stabbing again and again, avenged his mother and his twin. It is a curious reflection on the Age of Chivalry that not one of the actors in this discreditable drama showed any sign of observing modern standards of honour or fair play.

Henry of Trastámara was not the only bastard to rule Castile. ALVARO DE LUNA was an illegitimate member of one of Aragón's noblest families and, in accordance with the custom of those days, did not find his irregular birth a handicap. On the contrary, though his own talents made him the bosom friend of a king, it was his birth which enabled him to refer to his uncle, the Pope. For his father's brother had been Archbishop of Toledo and when he launched his illegitimate nephew into court circles he had become the Avignon Pope Benedict XIII. Spaniards claim that he founded St Andrew's University in Fife and he certainly drafted the statutes of the University of Salamanca. Alvaro came to the court of John II in 1409 at the age of eighteen, when the king was eight years old. From the beginning he exercised such fascination and established such an ascendancy over the young monarch that he became king in all but name for a period of thirty years. Along with the acquisition of enormous, some say uncountable, wealth he possessed himself of the two highest offices in the land, becoming High Constable of Castile and Master of Santiago. In the privileged position to which he had risen he need refuse himself nothing. And a man who had cowed the nobles of Castile and kept them harmless for three decades was not likely to be scared by stories of ill-starred jewels; the Girdle of Zobeida joined his huge treasure.

Meanwhile King John devoted himself to the life of a dilettante, for which he is invariably criticised; he is rarely given credit for raising the cultural status of the court of Castile to that of the French or Catalan civilisations. Perhaps his Plantagenet blood – he was the grandson of John of Gaunt – infused some originality into the dull Trastámara heritage. I fid it hard to blame him for having no interest in affairs of state: with Alvaro to do the work and keep the nobles in their place he could devote himself to the more enduring triumphs of the mind and he is still known for his delightful poems. His daughter Isabel lives in history but his family, his friends, his quarrelsome grandees, even Alvaro himself, are hardly known outside Spain. Though his grip on the kingdom slackened more than once, Alvaro de Luna always made his way back to power and Castile enjoyed a period of comparative peace. Fernán Pérez de Guzmán, the contemporary historian, describes him in his usual vivid way as a small man with a small face, but well built, a good horseman and skilled in arms; more important, he was well mannered and adept in debate. "He placed great value on his lineage, not remembering the humble and lowly descent of his mother".[6] His avarice impressed his biographer more than any other quality and he is said to have replied to a letter from a friend (urging moderation) with a Latin quotation from the Gospels: *Qui venerit ad me non ejiciam foras*, which he incorrectly rendered as "I will not reject that which cometh to me."

Alvaro's days were numbered when he arranged the King's second marriage, to the Portuguese princess who was to become the mother of Isabel the Catholic. Instead of the obedient nonentity he had expected, the new Queen soon showed herself independent, she allied herself with the resentful nobility and persuaded her husband to write the fateful order to his chief of police, Destúñiga, "I command that you attach the person of Don Alvaro de Luna, Master of Santiago, and if he defend himself that you kill him." Alvaro, however, was well protected by his retinue and matters reached a deadlock, resolved only when John II wrote a personal letter to his old friend, reproduced in the official chronicle, giving his royal word that he would receive injury to neither himself nor his property if he submitted. Strange that Alvaro should trust a Trastámara. To round off the catalogue of royal infamy I may add that when Alvaro, now a prisoner, sent a humble request for an interview, the King replied that he, Alvaro, had taught him never to speak to one whose arrest he had ordered; and when the King had dined he sent for Alvaro's keys and had all his valuables brought to him. Was he perhaps looking for the Scorpion Girdle? If so he was to be disappointed and it is tempting to attribute subsequent events to the King's chagrin.

It is not surprising to read that the subsequent trial, on a charge of having bewitched the King, was mere formality and that His

Mexuar a patio at the Alhambra in Granada.

Majesty himself signed the order for a public execution. But the nobles could not have realised that their public revenge on Alvaro would lower such esteem as their caste still commanded. A few more years of faction fighting and private brigandage, a state of affairs resembling the contemporary Wars of the Roses, and the Spanish nobles too would lose all but the illusion of political power. After his death they scrambled without restraint for the vacant offices and privileges – not the money, for the King had already taken care of that. There was a long search for the Girdle of Zobeida; it may have been unlucky but the King and Queen wanted it back. It was eventually discovered built into a vault under Alvaro's castle in Madrid, the stronghold of an insignificant town.

Alvaro died well. The chronicler describes his last morning; he heard mass and took the sacrament, ate a few mazard cherries and drank a cup of pure wine; even today many Spaniards dilute their table wine for ordinary occasions. Then, mounted on a mule (the perogative of nobility; common criminals rode an ass) he took part in his last procession, to the Plaza Ochavo, which still adjoins Valladolid's Plaza Mayor. The customary crier preceded him, repeating the sentence "for the misdeeds and disservices of this tyrant and usurper of the royal crown". Once he made a mistake and said ". . . services . . ." and Alvaro remarked, "Well said, my boy; this is how they repay me for my services." When the executioner approached with a cord Alvaro asked him what he wanted to do.

"Sir, I want to tie you hands with this cord."

"Don't do it like that"; and taking off a chain that he wore round his neck, "Tie me with this and I beg you to see that your dagger[7] is sharp, so that you may dispatch me quickly." Then he asked, "Tell me; that hook on the post up there, what is it there for?"

"That", said the executioner, "is so that when you have been beheaded, your head may be hung there."

"When I am beheaded", said the Master, "they can do what they like with my head and body."

If the Master of Santiago lived as well as he died, then he is the victim of defamation. What amazes me is the chronicler's account that follows: below the head of this millionaire, who had just given away a mule, a ring and his hat to a page, was placed a silver bowl for alms to pay for his funeral, "and in that basin was thrown a sufficiency. And when the three days had passed all the Brothers of Mercy came and took his body away in a litter and had it buried in a hermitage outside the town, which they call St Andrew's, where they are wont to bury all criminals; and after a few days he was taken thence to be buried in the Monastery of St Francis, which is inside the town. And when sufficient time had passed, his body with his head were taken to a most sumptuous chapel which he had ordered to be made in the great church of the city of Toledo; and thus ended all the glory of the Master and Constable Alvaro de Luna".

Except that you can still see the Chapel of the Constable in Toledo Cathedral, as I mentioned before, and in that sense his glory survives.

The Light House of San Sebastian on the Coast of Biscay.

The Castillo de Coca. The original structure was built by the Moors in 1400.

CHAPTER SEVEN

Founders of Empire

ISABEL LA CATOLICA

King John II of Castile, of the House of Trastámara, married twice. From the first union sprang, or rather shuffled, the strange figure of Enrique the Impotent; from the second an Alfonso who died in his teens and his sister Isabel, known in Spain (for Isabel – Elizabeth – is a common enough name) as la Catolica. Among the decayed remnants of once prosperous towns in Old Castile is one of the most remarkable – Madrigalde las Altas Torres, the birthplace of Isabel. Aprt from the beauty of its name (which has nothing to do with singing) the circle of its ruined *mudéjar* walls with their high towers still encloses the whole town, an indication that no expansion has taken place for six hundred years. In places the towers have kept their original height; elsewhere a shapeless stump rises from a heap of rubble or a line of humble cottages marks an original curtain wall.

When Isabel was three her father died and the kingdom devolved on her half-brother Enrique. Like his father, he was governed by his favourite and of course unpleasant stories were told to account for their affection. The favourite was Juan Pacheco, later Marquis of Villena, and though authors often repeat the story that he was of noble birth, the truth is that he and his uncle, the Archbishop of Toledo, were New Christians descended from the *converso* Jew Ruy Capón. On Enrique's accession to the throne his stepmother (the queen who had accomplished the downfall of Alvaro de Luna) retired with her children Alfonso and

117

Isabel to her castle at Arévolo. Here Isabel passed her formative years, learning the skills expected of a gentlewoman — all her life she was to occupy her rare moments of rest with exquisite needlework — and absorbing from her mother that almost fanatical devotion to the Faith which either prompted or cloaked the important decisions of her reign. Her mother was meanwhile lapsing into a state of melancholic insanity, not, as is often said, because of frustration and solitude, but rather through that hereditary taint which produced madness in Isabel's daughter Juana and eccentric behaviour, to say the least, in some of her descendants.

After six years of marriage the second wife of Enrique "the Impotent" produced a daughter. The court favourite at the time was called Beltrán de la Cueva and the baby, though christened Juana, was and still is known as La Beltraneja. Many believe that the smear was thought up and spread by the previous favourite Juan Pacheco. After the passage of centuries it is even more difficult to ascribe paternity; but one should remember first that Enrique was allegedly potent with mistresses, and secondly that the earliest recorded attempt at artificial insemination concerned the Queen as recipient and Enrique as donor. We shall never know whether the experiment was a success, but the story raises the intriguing question whether Enrique's disability may have been sterility due to anatomical causes, rather than impotence.

We have seen how Isabel's extreme youth was spent; even as a child her main concern was to thwart attempts at using her as a pawn in power politics. It is unnecessary for us to follow these in detail or to guess why Enrique is said to have alternately acknowledged and repudiated the legitimacy of La Beltraneja. Once Isabel was promised in marriage to Pedro Girón, brother of Juan Girón and Master of Calatrava; it is told that she spent a day and a night on her knees praying for divine help and that the aspiring groom was smitten with a fatal quinsy on his way to claim his fifteen-year-old bride. Did this deliverance from marriage to a New Christian, the answer to prayer, play its part in Isabel's later policy?

Two years after this episode her brother Alfonso died suddenly and she withdrew to a convent at Avila. Here she was sought out by Pacheco's uncle, the Archbishop of Toledo, proposing that she should take her late brother's place as a figurehead for a revolt of the nobles. With commendable prudence she refused, demonstrating that submission to established regal authority which she was to exact from others after her accession. Of course her correct behaviour to her half-brother Enrique did not extend to the unfortunate Beltraneja, whose faction she and her husband (to anticipate) finally defeated in 1479. Meanwhile she kept away from the crowd of degenerates who swarmed round the throne and, when ordered to live at the court, remained unsullied by the general licence that prevailed there. It is difficult for us to imagine her feelings after leaving the quiet of Arévalo and Avila, when transplanted to a court whose principal characters were the unsavoury king, the unscrupulous Pacheco and the unspeakable Beltrán de la Cueva, vain as a peacock and revelling in the dubious notoriety of Her Majesty's bed.

In 1469, before succeeding to the throne, indeed before her succession was assured, Isabel of Castile married her second cousin Ferdinand, heir apparent to the throne of Aragón. In this way, and at long last, the unity and grandeur of the greater part of Spain was achieved. Isabel and Ferdinand built a mighty edifice through the exercise of courage, constancy and cruelty; devotion and duplicity; heroism and hypocrisy. It is customary to attribute the nobler qualities to the Queen, and chivalrous historians write as though Ferdinand was responsible for every reprehensible deed; but many of them must have had at least the tacit approval of Isabel for we are told that she never allowed Ferdinand to dictate matters of policy. On the contrary, von Popielow, a visitor from Silesia, who met the royal family in Seville in 1484, wrote: "I saw then that the King is servant to the Queen, because he has her on his right hand . . . so marked is this that the nobility fears the Queen more than the King."[1] He goes on to describe the King's subservience and to emphasise that he can do nothing without her permission. She reads all his letters, and we cannot blame her if it was to ascertain that Ferdinand regarded his marriage vows as lightly as other solemn promises. It is noteworthy that, even in her will, Isabel excluded her husband from inheriting the crown of Castile.

In accordance with custom, each sovereign chose as an emblem an object that began with the partner's initial. Thus Ysabel (as she spelled her name) chose *flechas* (arrows) for "Fernando" and he the *yugo* or yoke.[2] Their joint motto was a jingle that we see displayed on many a building:

> *Tanto monta, monta tanto*
> *Ysabel y Don Fernando*

signifying that the eminence of each was *tantamount* to that of
the other.

The young pair was faced immediately with three major
problems. The first was that of the succession of Castile, for the
King of Portugal supported the claim of La Beltraneja. The
ensuing war ended in a victory for Isabel and Ferdinand. The
second problem was posed by the Castilian nobles, who had never
resumed obedience since the death of Alvaro de Luna, sixteen
years before. Thanks to Isabel's inflexible will, the prestige of the
crown was again established, principally by rigorous application of
the law; in this the *Hermandad*, whose headquarters we saw in
Toledo, played a large part. The high towers of proud nobles were
lopped off leaving them defenceless before retribution. In England
the Wars of the Roses achieved the same result at the same time,
but more by suicidal strife than by royal authority.

The third threat was poverty. Enrique the Impotent, ably
supported by his courtiers, had emptied the royal treasury; over a
hundred mints had been set up, most of them in private hands,
and inevitably the coinage was debased. My own opinion, which
you need not share, is that the great achievements of the
remainder of the reign of Isabel and Ferdinand were prompted by
the perpetual threat of insolvency. It certainly seems likely that it
played a part in the three dramatic events of the wonderful year
1492: the conquest of Granada, the expulsion of the Jews and the
discovery of America.

In the fight against financial collapse one institution was of
supreme importance. The Inquisition, though well established in
the Western world, was new to Castile and was different in some
respects. It was approved, reluctantly and after much hesitation,
by Pope Sixtus IV in 1478; the reluctance was due to the demand
that the Spanish Inquisition should be under royal and not papal
control. This was in keeping with the aim of the Catholic
Sovereigns – unified command over a unified country. The results
of their policy amply justified the means they used. That the
Spanish Inquisition was run as a lucrative business is usually

The Catholic Sovereigns, Ferdinand and Isabel.

played down, if mentioned at all, and Durant,[3] for instance, states that Ferdinand refused bribes from rich victims begging him to overrule the inquisitors; but why should he accept a bribe of part of the victim's wealth when the latter's condemnation would ensure that all of it became the property of the state? However sympathetically we try to view the stamping out of heresy and the saving of souls, the profit motive keeps intruding. It is easily discerned in the war against Granada. Apart from the ostensible cause, the witholding of tribute by the Moslems, there were cities to be won, rich plains – the *vegas* – to support the loyal nobles and ransoms to swell the treasury. But artillery was essential and the latest and best weapons had to be bought from the Venetians; the lombards, designed to throw marble cannon balls but also used in this campaign with iron ones, were bought through Barcelona and Valencia brokers, and it was for this and not for Columbus' voyage that Isabel is said to have pawned her jewels or promised to pawn them, if needed.

After the execution of Alvaro de Luna physicians were called in to prescribe for King John, sick with remorse; in desperation a soothsayer was eventually summoned. He advised the King to get rid of the sinister Girdle of Zobeida. The jewels were removed from their settings and given to nobles or sold to merchants. Only

Madrigal de las Altas Torres.

the two giant emeralds remained, for their value was beyond the means of the usual buyer. Now, when Isabel needed money so desperately, they were sold to a Genoese Jew who knew that a bankrupt country is the place to find bargains. The emeralds went to Italy. From thereto Portugal was a fairly obvious move, for Henry the Navigator's captains were slaking Europe's thirst for gold and Portugal was the great market for precious stones, spices and other products of the East.

The war as a whole was fought by both sides with horrifying ruthlessness, occasionally punctuated by an act of chivalry. After the capture of Málaga Ferdinand worthily sustained his reputation for perfidy. True, the Malagueños had resisted with deplorable obstinacy and could hardly expect terms; many Christians urged that the whole population be put to the sword, but, as Irving tells us "the human heart of Isabella revolted at such sanguinary counsels: she insisted that their triumph should not be disgraced by cruelty"[4] and she persuaded Ferdinand to permit the ransom of *those citizens who could afford it*. How this was done makes interesting reading: being told that the citizens of Málaga might hide their valuables, Ferdinand sentenced them all to slavery but allowed them to ransom themselves for an exorbitant sum, admitting their valuables in part payment. When the agreed time had expired and the full ransom had not been produced the Catholic Sovereigns found themselves in possession of all the movable property, half the ransom and all the persons of the citizens of Málaga. Thus, in a crusade, you *can* have your cake and eat it, and win esteem at the same time.

With their supplies of men and materials cut off by the fall of Málaga, the destruction of their fertile fields and a perpetual civil war raging at home, the fall of Granada was a foregone conclusion. The history of the ten years' war is marked, as you might expect, by the vigour and resolution of its female participants. On the Christian side Isabel performed miracles of organisation, herself supervising the well-being of her troops in difficult mountain territories and amid appalling climatic contrasts. Of the Moslems, the most indomitable was Boabdil's mother Aixa, whose well-known reproof to the men who wept on leaving their earthly paradise of Granada is typical of Spanish womanhood.

The treaty of capitulation gave most generous terms, including a cash payment to the Moorish king and the guarantee of freedom of worhsip in their own mosques. What, then, of the high ideals of the crusade, of the eradication of the Mohammedan heresy? Have patience. Boabdil, the deposed King of Granada, soon tired of his token kingdom in the Alpujarras and was tricked into withdrawing to North Africa, he sold his estate, as allowed in the treaty, to the conquerors, who cheated him of part of the price. Isabel's saintly confessor, the *converso* Hernando de Talavera, was made Archbishop of Granada and began the task of conversion with tact and sympathy. After eight years the results were so meagre that Cardinal Ximemez de Cisneros was sent to help. Strangely, for one who founded the important University of Alcalá, he began by copying Almanzor and burning thousands of Arabic books. His methods were effective: among his stratagems was the ringing of church bells loudly enough to drown the muezzins' call to prayer. By this and other means the Moors were goaded into revolt, defeated and then faced with the choice of exile or conversion. Most chose the latter and by 1502 there were no overt Moslems, only Christian *moriscos*, ripe for the big squeeze – the Spanish Inquisition.

This institution had to pay its own salaries and expenses from fines and confiscations, and its share was only a small one. I take it the reader has a fair idea of its methods – the secret accusation, the withholding from the prisoner of the very nature of the charge, the anonymity of the witnesses – and of the years that could be spent in solitary confinement with repeated examinations by the inquisitors who had records of the answers at every previous questioning. Finally of the torture, applied to both sexes and at all ages, the records giving the limits of ten and ninety-seven years. My object in touching on this revolting subject is to point out that confession, by whatever means obtained, meant condemnation and confiscation of all property. This had already been sequestered at the moment of arrest and from it the expenses of keeping the victim in prison had also been deducted. It may be true, and has often been maintained, that the Spanish Inquisition, judged by the standards of the times, was neither cruel nor unjust in its procedures and its penalties. But most of us find it impossible to judge by those standards.

The jurisdiction of the Spanish Inquisition, it must be remembered, extended only to Christians suspected of heresy. Those most suspect, often with reason, were Moslems and Jews who had embraced Christianity to save themselves and their families from death during the waves of persecution that every now and then swept through Spain. Professing Jews and Moslems, whatever disabilities they might suffer in other respects, were immune from the attentions of the Holy Office. It was the *conversos*, therefore, who attracted the interest of the Inquisition and who, being a comparatively wealthy class, could be expected to keep the home fires burning. For a condemned heretic – a Catholic who had relapsed into his former religion – could be burned alive or after a merciful strangulation, or in effigy if he had escaped the country; his remains could be produced for the *auto de fé* if he had died under torture and pushed in a wheelbarrow to the *quemadero*, or place of burning, like the still living survivors who could no longer walk. In all cases he, or his effigy or his bones, had been condemned and his property now belonged to the state.

The trouble, of course, was to pick out the *conversos* who could profitably be investigated without risk of protest from influential quarters. There had been so much intermarriage between money and blue blood that a borderline was difficult to establish. Sir Charles Petrie declares not only that the financial profits from the Inquisition were considerable, but that it was a useful threat to hold over the nobles, whose Christian blod was seldom pure. At this late date it is difficult to decide on the truth of statements that are repeated by one writer after another. Archbishop Talavera, the Queen's confessor, was the son of converted Jewish parents; Tomás de Torquemada, a notorious leader in the fight against heresy, was also alleged to be of Jewish descent, and the same taint is said to have affected the Enriquez family, from which Ferdinand the Catholic was descended on his mother's side. To illustrate the complexities of the problem I must mention that Isabel's best friend, Beatriz de Bobadilla, married into a *converso* family and that the war against Granada was largely financed by Jewish loans, the actual management of finances being in the hands of two Jewish members of the council, Abraham Senior and Isaac Abarbanel. It is interesting to note that the *marrano*, or secret Jew, whom Borrow met in the 1830s was called Abarbenel, which is similar enough to suggest identity, and that he referred to the long dead Catholic Sovereigns as "Fernando the Accursed and Jezebel".

Historians have exercised much ingenuity in explaining the edict of 1492, decreeing the expulsion by 30th July of all Jews who had not in the meantime embraced Christianity. The usual explanation is that the Catholic Sovereigns, flushed with the victorious outcome of their crusade, now wanted to unite the whole country in religion as well as government. Had they forgotten the treaty they had just signed with the Moors, pledging themselves to respect all their religious institutions and buildings? Surely they were not already contemplating breaking their royal word? However that may be, the edict went forth and within four months the Jews of Spain had to leave, forbidden to carry money, precious metal or stones. They were forced to pay all taxes due before the end of the year but had to leave the collection of money owed them in the hands of Christians. Among these debts were some of the loans the Catholic Sovereigns had raised for the prosecution of the war against Granada. One can sense the strain on the shaky economy of the conquerors when they had paid King Boabdil the first instalment of the 30,000 gold castellanos agreed on in the treaty and the arrears of pay of the mercenaries they were now dismissing; among these were 2,000 Swiss pikemen who gave and expected the full value of their services. A final reason for the edict of expulsion was the hope that numbers of Jews would elect to remain as New Christians – actually only about

50,000 did so — thus providing the Inquisition with more souls to save and property to confiscate. In order to make quite sure of their prey the *conversos* were not allowed to leave Spain, while the unconverted were forbidden to remain.

The financial results of their efforts were meagre but in 1494 the Spanish Borgia Pope Alexander VI conferred on Isabel and Ferdinand the proud title of "Catholic Sovereigns". That of "Most Christian" was first suggested but passed over because it had already been bestowed on the kings of France (who were soon to ally themselves with the Turks against the Spanish); when it became Henry VIII of England's turn, as a reward for his opposition to Luther, "Defender of the Faith" was the best that could be contrived.

But before all this Isabel helped to mould history by a decision far more important than the conquest of Granada or the exile of defenceless citizens; she was instrumental, albeit with hesitation and parsimony, in the discovery of America. The importance of the voyages of Columbus cannot be overestimated and it is only right that the New World should have a country, several provinces and numerous towns named after the hero. To the foreigner the Spanish version of his name may at first seem strange and thousands have passed through the Panama Canal without recognising the explorer's names in the twin towns of Cristóbal and Colón.

It is almost a miracle that Spain was the sponsor of the Genoese sailor who had been rejected, first by Portugal and then by Spain herself. Columbus brought forward his proposal at the worst possible time, when Isabel and Ferdinand had won a civil war, repelled a French threat, broken the power of the nobles, restored order in a united Spain and embarked on a long and costly war against Granada, all in ten years. Furthermore, ideas of expansion were apt to be fixed on the French border, in the disputed provinces of Cerdagne and Roussillon, Sicily and Southern Italy, to which the crown of Aragón was intimately tied, and North Africa, whence any new Moorish or Turkish invasion must come.

Bu t just as lack of money was a stumbling block to Columbus' enterprise, so its need was an incentive. At this time more and more gold was coming into circulation and the demand in Europe increasing; countries such as Spain and England were suffering from its lack, while Portugal was steadily increasing her reserves from the Guinea coast. Columbus shared the now common knowledge that the earth was a sphere and, hoping to find a new route to the Indies, crossed the Atlantic eight times and died fourteen years later without an inkling that he had discovered a new continent. His obsession, for that is what it amounted to, may have begun on a voyage to Iceland in 1477; here he learned of the colonies established in Greenland by the Norsemen and heard traditions of Norse expeditions to the New World, called Vinland in the sagas, and which he would believe formed part of Asia.

It is unnecessary to repeat the story of his protracted dealings with the court of Spain. Of one thing we are sure: Columbus did not underestimate his own value and was determined to wager his life for nothing less than social standing and the means to maintain it. At Santa Fé, the city built to house the besiegers of Granada, Columbus witnessed the final surrender and was then interviewed by the court. He apparently succeeded, as Prescott terms it, in stimulating the cupidity of his audience and, himself almost as devout as Isabel, held out the prospect of extending the empire of the Cross.

All would have been settled had Columbus been prepared to bargain. As it was, negotiations were broken off and he left with the intention of approaching France or England. He had gone only four miles when a message of recall overtook him at Pinos Puente, some say on the very bridge where a chapel stands to this day.

The bridge at Pinos Puente

Much ink has flowed in attempting to explain this hasty change of mind, the favourite explanation being an offer to finance the expedition on the part of the *converso* treasurer Luis de Santángel. The solution I offer is that someone remembered that the port of Palos, because of an act of piracy, had been condemned to maintain two caravels for a year for the public service. Negotiations were resumed and, as an example of the poverty or parsimony of the Sovereigns, Columbus was promised an extra eighth of the profits in return for contributing a proportionate part of the expenses. From then on the expedition was energetically and economically organised; stores were bought duty-free and reluctant sailors were tempted by immunity from criminal prosecution. The total cost of the expedition is said to have been only 17,000 florins, a sum so trifling that the Queen had no need to pawn her jewels.

Palos de la Frontera, the port from which the 100-ton *Santa María* and the two felucca-rigged caravels sailed, has been abandoned by the receding waters of the Río Tinto but you may still visit the Franciscan monastery of La Rábida, where Columbus was so hospitably entertained and supported. Columbus sailed from Palos on 3rd August, 1492 and returned on 15th March, 1493; in a meadow are rusty iron rings which are shown to the credulous as having secured the three ships, though in fact they rode at anchor in the river.

For the site of his triumphal reception you must go to Barcelona where, on the steps of the Chapel of St Agatha, near the Cathedral,the Catholic Sovereigns did him the unprecedented honour of rising as he came forward to bring them the momentous news. At the harbour end of the great thoroughfare, the Ramblas, is the towering monument to Columbus, and not far away, made fast to the quay, is a replica of his flagship, the *Santa María*. Strolling round the tiny vessel you must try to imagine the late afternoon of 11th October, when floating vegetation and a stick or two persuaded even the near-mutinous crew that land was near. We can only guess at his emotions when it was sighted and again when he, the unknown visionary, sat at the right hand of kings.

But his glory diminished, even during his lifetime. Isabel was loyal to her admiral when the inevitable reaction occurred and word went about that there was little profit in the new lands. Even when he was found to be enslaving the natives, she was his champion and is said to have wept when she saw him sent back in chains, though another account states that she ordered him to be set free long before they met again. Her character was, in fact, remarkable and she shines above her contemporaries for devotion to duty, resolution and loyalty. Where she fell short of our ideals we should blame her mother and her religious advisers, who had infused in her the belief that Moslem and Jewish heretics were a distinct species, for whom no pity need be felt and to whom no promises were binding. It is incorrect to say, as some have, that she had no vindictiveness in her character, for what else prompted her to reprove the Pope for his humane reception of the unfortunate citizens whom she had driven out penniless? Let us

The Royal Steps outside the Chapel of St Agatha, in the Plaza del Rey in Barcelona.

regard her bigotry as an acquired quality, an obedience to her advisers comparable to her resignation to God's will, when her children and grandchildren died and she saw the inheritance of all she had built up passing to a demented daughter. There are many who retain the belief that Spain is still a bigoted and backward country. I would remind them that modern Spanish as well as foreign authors stress the two great mistakes of Isabel's reign: the institution of the Spanish Inquisition and the expulsion of the Jews. Educated Spaniards usually agree.

Seville Cathedral, the largest Gothic building in the world, is the setting for the last act, for here is the sumptuous tomb that holds the remains of Columbus, expressing all the triumph and homage that he enjoyed for so short a time. A few steps away, in the floor of the nave, is the grave of his son Fernando; of him Baron de Bourgoing, plagiarised by Richard Ford, wrote, "He would have been considered a great man had he had a less famous father."[5] The gift of a new world, in return for a modest outlay, is acknowledged by an inscription on both tombs:

A CASTILLA Y A LEON
MUNDO NUEBO DIO COLON

Gabia la Grande and Vega of Granada.

CHAPTER EIGHT

The Golden Century and After

While Castile was securing her hold on the New World Aragón was pursuing her old Mediterranean aims. Thanks to the genius and loyalty of Gonzalo Fernández de Córdoba, "The Great Captain", Spain added the kingdom of Naples to that of Sicily, thus extending her rule to include the southern half of Italy. Isabel died in 1504, her husband in 1516, allegedly from too earnest an attempt to ensure the succession by his second marriage (to Germaine de Foix). It thus passed to Juana, married to Philip the Fair of Burgundy. In her the eccentricities of her grandmother and elder sister declared themselves as frank insanity and as *Juana la Loca* ("Crazy Jane") she is still known.

CHARLES V, Juana's elder son, was born in 1500. He inherited not only Spain, where (at Villaviciosa) he set foot for the first time in 1517, and the Spanish possessions of Sicily and southern Italy, but also Burgundy, the Low Countries and Austria or, in other words, the Hapsburg slice of the European cake. In 1521 he wisely handed Austria over to his brother Ferdinand but he more than compensated for this lost portion by the vast territories his explorers carved out in the New World and by further conquests in Italy and North Africa.

That he ruled the first empire on which the sun never set[1] is of little importance He learned how not to rule by the revolt of the *comuneros.* Interestingly, the uprising was centred on Castile, the heart of Spain, and was the protest of squirearchy against

131

foreign influence. Had it succeeded, the eventual decline of Spain might have been postponed. Though negligible in battle the leaders, Juan Bravo, Juan de Padilla and Francisco Maldonado, behaved like heroes on the scaffold and are so regarded by Spaniards today, witness the statue to the first-named in his native town of Segovia and the imaginative painting of Gisbert, illustrating Padilla's last words, "Señor Juan Bravo, yesterday was the day for fighting like knights; today for dying like Christians." From them Charles learned his lesson: the revolt was not against him but against his absence and his reliance on Flemish favourites. He decided to be a Spaniard, learned the Castilian language and appointed Spanish officials. The *comunero* revolt gives us an example, not only of Spanish bravery, but of Spanish discord. Brother fought, literally, against brother. Padilla's was an officer in the loyalist army; in another family, Pedro Laso de Vega, an elder brother, was a *comunero* while a younger, Garci, fought and was wounded in the service of Charles, the King-Emperor. We met him briefly in Toledo as Garcilaso, the poet of rare and delicate sensibility.

Charles' other mistake was more serious. Like Alfonso el Sabio he wanted the crown of the Holy Roman Empire and he bought it. Thus, though he was the first Charles to rule Spain, he is generally known as Carlos V, the fifth emperor of that name. For the title, which served only to embroil him in religious wars and may have contributed to the grievances of the *comuneros*, he squandered the wealth of Spain. To ensure peace at home while he pursued fame abroad he entrusted much of the government of Spain to the lesser nobility; the *hidalgos* (more correctly *hijosdalgo*) then ensured their own prosperity by sheep farming. Arable became pasture and consequently wheat had to be imported; in an attempt to remedy this the vital wool industry was crippled by well-meaning legislation. Thus the *hijosdalgo*, as feeble-minded a class as their supreme example, Don Quixote, gnawed at Spain's roots while her branches were spreading over and beyond the known world.

Charles' happiest days were those which followed his marriage in 1526 to Princess Elizabeth of Portugal. Accounts of the sumptuous wedding, which took place in the splendid Hall of the Ambassadors of Seville's Alcázar, mention two great emeralds that the bride brought in a pendant. They were the emeralds of Zobeida's Girdle. A year later we find him unable to restrain his own army, of which at least half consisted of German Protestants; Rome was sacked and the Pope taught a lesson, for Spanish kings were apt to be ultra-catholic and anti-papal at the same time.

We can hardly blame Charles for his greatest mistake: while the country was impoverished by war and the bribing of German electors, gold and silver began to pour in from America; he was not to know that, far from solving his difficulties, it would increase them. The effect was comparable to the results of printing more paper money to stave off bankruptcy, or giving sugar to a diabetic. And so his son and successor, Philip II, inherited a virtually bankrupt state with the obligation to wage expensive war in the defence of his religion.

Charles was one of the few powerful rulers who retired voluntarily; you may still see his suite at the Monastery of Yuste, set among the scenic mountains of Extremadura. Two episodes mark his passing: he audibly regretted that he had not broken his word when he gave Luther a safe-conduct; perhaps he remembered how Harpsburg agents had caught John Huss by this despicable trick and had him burned alive. And the emeralds of Zobeida's Girdle were sent to his son Philip by a trusty messenger. On his tomb were carved the words, "Between Villaviciosa and Yuste he conquered an empire for Spain." Its financial state is not mentioned.

PHILIP II is seen by Spanish historians as the leader under whom their country reached its highest peak of glory; but the facts show that his ambitions were thwarted in every field. More devout than his father, he met with opposition from the German nobles when Charles V wanted to nominate him King of Rome, a preliminary to the title of Holy Roman Emperor. More dedicated to the mechanics of ruling, it was in his reign that Spanish influence in the Low Countries began to decline. More enterprising in the task of stemming the Turkish menace in the Mediterranean, his fleet and that of Venice triumphed at Lepanto in 1571, only for the Turks to seize Tunis a year later. In fact the only result of the "decisive" battle to arouse our interest was Philip's present to the victor, his half-brother Don Juan of Austria — the emeralds from Zobeida's Girdle.

The truth is that "El Prudente", as he is called, took on too much for one man to manage, however dedicated. Wherever he turned he was faced with impossible tasks. After the death of his second wife, Queen Mary of England, he needed her successor Elizabeth on the throne as a counter to the powerful Guises of France; Elizabeth used his support, helped the Protestants in the Low Countries and did nothing to check her captains in their careers of piracy and of smuggling negro slaves into the Spanish colonies. After he eventually accepted the Guise faction as allies in the great task of sustaining Catholicism, he was soon to see the Protestant Henry of Navarre change his liturgy, but not his beliefs, in order to inherit the throne of France. Sitting in his office in the Escorial he tried to exercise control over the whole known world; now he would be writing to the King of Poland about the menace of Lutheranism, now discussing the projected assassination of Queen Elizabeth with his London ambassador; and he would spend hours reading and annotating the minutes of the Councils of State. With him bureaucracy and centralisation and their inevitable train of delays and mistakes, entered Spain. They have survived as the only bequest of Philip the Prudent.

Poor Philip. Bankruptcies were not his only problem. As champion of the Catholic faith he had to fight, not only revolt in the Netherlands and the Turkish menace, but a serious uprising of the *moriscos* (Moslem *conversos*) in Andalucía. He felt that he had some sort of claim on England by being the widower of "Bloody Mary". Queen Elizabeth rejected him as a suitor and not only openly helped the rebellious Dutch but finally executed Mary, Queen of Scots, who was pledged to support Spanish interests. All the prestige won by the gallant Spaniards at Lepanto was lost when the equally brave crews of the Armada were defeated by the captains of England and their own ship-chandlers. The dreadful return voyage round the north of Scotland through storms and against head winds is an epic in itself. Taking into account the shortage of water, the number of sick and wounded and the battered state of their vessels, it is a tribute to Spanish seamanship that all forty-four ships clearing the coast of Ireland eventually got home.

The following year England thought to take advantage of the Armada's defeat. On 4th May 1589 Drake appeared before Corunna and landed an assault party. The breach was made, the attackers reached the summit of the wall and there was talk of capitulation when María Pita, who had just seen her husband killed, snatched the sword from the hand of an exhausted countryman and with it killed the English standard-bearer, whose banner then formed a rallying point for the garrison. Her actions and her words which, we are led to believe, were appropriate to a Galician fishwife, shamed the defenders; the breach was cleared and the English fleet sailed off on their main assignment, to restore a pretender to the Portuguese throne that now belonged to Philip. This too was a failure.

Philip has always been cast as the villain. When his eldest son died under restraint Philip was considered the murderer and the boy's stepmother the cause. The natural death of the deformed, perverted young lunatic was greedily seized upon, altered and adapted as part of the Black Legend of Spain, in the form that it takes, for instance. in Schiller's play and Verdi's opera *Don Carlos.* We are too apt to forget the Philip whose smiling portrait in miniature adorns a manuscript in the town hall of Alora, the Philip who was vexed if the gardener forgot his morning bunch of roses, the Philip who loved to listen to the nightingales in the patios of the Escorial. Did you know that nightingales used to nest in the courtyards of that great grey, grim palace-monastery that Herrera finished in 1684? Think of it next time you walk through the granite corridors. But when you come to the marble Christ that Benvenuto Cellini made, remember also that the enigmatic Philip tied his own handkerchief round the loins for modesty's sake; and that he ordered a painting of St Maurice from El Greco for the chapel of the Escorial and then refused it for being "futuristic". After his death in 1598 the decline of Spain became apparent. As I have remarked, it set in over half a century earlier, when bad housekeeping led to bankruptcy. His successors entrusted the affairs of the nation to a series of incompetent and self-seeking favourites, until at the end of the seventeenth century the House of Hapsburg perished from inanition and inbreeding. That it lasted so long is remarkable; Philip III, for instance, was a seventh child and succeeded only through the premature death of four brothers. Luckily for Spain, her common people were of tougher fibre.

But enough of emperors and kings. We get an idea of the harm they can do by Philip III's edict of 1609. decreeing the expulsion of the *moriscos* – Christians in name and largely Spanish by descent – Spain thus ridding herself of her most skilled and industrious artisans. The Spain you should see was largely the work of an astonishing Renaissance, if I may use the term loosely. Late but brilliant, it flowered more luxuriantly as kings became more incompetent, reflecting and in many cases outshining that of Italy. In representational art alone, sixteenth- and seventeenth-century Spain numbers its giants by the score: El Greco, the Berruguetes, Martínez Montañés, Ribera, Zurbarán, Alonso Cano, Murillo and Velázquez are but a handful that have been raised to the pinnacle of popular esteem from among the mass of their peers. In literature, contemporary Spain can be challenged only by Shakespeare, for Garcilaso de la Vega, Góngora, Lope de Vega and the matchless Cervantes were all before Milton's time. As the ponderous, rusty machinery of absolute, centralised rule was creaking to a halt, the arts despairingly tried to save its face. Calderón de la Barca was still writing about honour and duty when the words had become meaningless in the Spanish court, long after Cervantes had "smiled Spain's chivalry away." And while the rottenness was percolating through the ranks, until the invincible Spanish infantry were annihilated at Rocroi in 1643, mediaeval formality survived with a thousand useless vanities. So-and-so was addressed as "cousin" by the king while such-and-such were allowed to remain covered in the royal presence. A horse once ridden by the king might never again be mounted by another and, *mutatis mutandis*, no one might marry the king's discarded mistress.

The Catholic faith, destined to spread the light of knowledge in countries still undiscovered, was facing its greatest threat. Happily, a blend of mysticism and common sense arose in Spain, first with Loyola, then with St Teresa and her pupil St John of the Cross. Through them and many others Catholicism became more than a formula; by providing what humanity needed, the practical, disciplined mystics made Spain the spearhead of the Counter-Reformation. Brother Luis de León proved that religion need not be divorced from rational thinking. He differed from Maimonides, Averroes and St Thomas Aquinas, who strove to reconcile religion with the world; instead, he saw the world as the unworthy step by which, with the help of music and understanding, his heaven could be reached.

No account of Spain's rise to supremacy would be complete without a mention of her explorers and colonisers. With a handful of men she acquired extensive footholds in the Americas; if you feel that fighting men are unproductive and unworthy to be classed with the builders of civilisation; remember Garcilaso de la Vega, the beloved poet, whose sonnets were read avidly throughout Europe; he died aged thirty-three leading the assault on Le Muy. Alonso Cano killed his man in a duel. Cervantes was maimed at the Battle of Lepanto, having left his bunk of sickness to fight on deck, and Calderón fought in more than one campaign. Lope de Vega, the most prolific poet and playwright the world has seen, was a member of the Armada.

And some who have no claim to immortality in the arts may also live in our memory for their heroism. Cortés, who conquered Mexico and Guatemala — the former alone is four times the size of Spain — found time to serve under the Great Captain in Italy and Charles V before Algiers. Leading his tiny army into the unknown interior, he first burned their ships at Vera Cruz, in case any were faint-hearted enough to think of returning home. Pizarro, who conquered Peru with a handful of men, was one of the bravest villains who ever lived. Balboa was the first to look on the Pacific and De Soto not only colonised Florida but explored as far as the Mississippi. All these were men of Extremadura, a harsh land, fit mother of heroes. In 1544 Orellana crossed the Andes, as the Incas had done before him, and led his party down the Amazon over an uncharted 2000 miles, through lands of fever and poisoned arrows, now exposed to scorching heat, now in the perpetual twilight of vast forests, where even their direction could no longer be determined; he knew only that somewhere, some time, they ought to come out in the Atlantic. De Elcano accompanied Magellan as far as the Philippines, where the latter was killed, then sailed on westward. The first to circumnavigate the earth, he survived storms, hunger, thirst and scurvy, arriving in Spain with seventeen men of the original 280. He accomplished the feat about sixty years before Francis Drake in the *Golden Hind.*

The list could be endless, but may fittingly close with mention of two priests, of whom the first was Bartholomew de las Casas. His father had accompanied Columbus in his second voyage in 1493. He himself sailed in 1502 as a simple colonist. In 1511 he took Holy Orders and from then on declared himself champion of the ill-treated Indian. Like many another, he painted a colourful, rather than a realistic, picture, but thanks to his persistence and the support of Cardinal Cisneros, he was declared "Universal

Protector of the Indians". To prove that the Indian could be made a useful citizen by pacific means, he founded a monastery and colony at Cumaná, where he lavished gifts and friendship on the noble savage. The Indians responded by attacking and destroying it. Nevertheless Bartholomew de las Casas persisted; he crossed the Atlantic fourteen times – no mean feat for those days – and spent the rest of his ninety-two years largely in composing polemics defending his theory. His memory has survived the fierce attacks of his opponents and he is known today as "The Apostle of the Indians". History is the supreme humorist. It was Brother Bartholomew who introduced Negro slaves into America, so that creatures of a supposedly different species could release the Indian from the degradation of slavery. Apparently he had not met Juan de Valladolid, a contemporary Negro administrator of Seville. A century later our second priest appears, the Catalan Jesuit St Peter Claver, who eased the hardships of the Negro slaves in this life and ensured their salvation in the next. The Apostle of the Negroes.

Bartholomew outlived contemporary Indians and Spaniards with only the pen for a weapon and the breviary for a shield. Though he captured no native emperor and brought home neither gold nor silver he deserves to rank with the *conquistadores* who never refused to fight against odds of a hundred to one.

With thinkers and doers like these one would imagine that the Spanish Empire would have time to enjoy her supremacy. But her kings made sure that it would be brief, by systematic inbreeding and thorough neglect of their duties. Their favourites had none of Alvaro de Luna's efficiency, only his greed and ambition. In 1643 the catastrophic Battle of Rocroi saw the end of the Spanish infantry's supremacy, which had lasted nearly a century and a half. They and their allies were out-generalled by the Great Condé but none could deprive them of their glory. They died to a man, rank by rank, their leader Enriquez Acevedo de Toledo in the chair from which he commanded in the forefront. He was aged eighty-three.

Now Spain's sun was setting, though her western additions allowed her to enjoy the evening rays for a while. When the Hapsburgs died out the Bourbons came in and, with the exception of Charles III, showed themselves increasingly stupid and treacherous. It is Charles IV and his promiscuous wife who are caricatured for all time by Goya, in the guise of a court portrait. When he was still heir presumptive his wife begged him to ask the King to recall one of her lovers; Charles III turned away in disgust, saying, "Quiet, you idiot! Let him go! How simple you are!" And simple he was. Charles IV was not a complacent husband, merely a stupid one. He is reported to have said, "We, the crowned heads, have this advantage over others: that our honour, as they call it, is safe; for suppose that queens were as much bent on mischief as some of their sex, where could they find emperors and kings to flirt with, eh?"

Indirectly it was the Queen's lubricity that procured Napoleon's downfall. Her lover, Godoy, became virtual dictator and through him French troops got a foothold in Spain. Napoleon himself attributed his collapse to the combination of Spanish and British resistance that kept a large part of his army immobilised throughout the Peninsular War. To claim pre-eminence for one or other partner (and the Portuguese played their part too) is to waste energy. Wellington excelled in strategy and caution, the Spanish in tenacity. As we are concerned with the latter let me remind you of the siege of Gerona, whose citizens defended the mediaeval walls against the French as resolutely as the men and women of Zaragoza.

The most vivid account I know of the great second siege is that of Pérez Galdós in his novel entitled *Gerona*. Here is an extract, dealing with the last days of the siege, when a cat for two dollars was just a memory of the good old days; when the doctor offered a suite of furniture for one kitten with which to prepare a meal for his daughter, a nervous wreck from the previous siege; when he fought like a maniac with his companion for the corpse of a rat:

> "The street of La Forca, which leads to the Cathedral, was a horrible sump, a narrow, gloomy ditch where humans were lying, waiting to be rescued or killed. We went in and sorted out the live and half-alive, the dead and half-dead, dragging them to the steps of the Cathedral where less foetid air might play on them. The Cathedral could not accommodate more patients and the square had been converted into an open-air hospital."

One glance at the stupendous flight of a hundred broad steps gives you an idea of how they looked, packed with men and women dying of starvation, disease of wounds.

Picture those whose endurance is enshrined in Gerona's fame. Regular troops numbered probably no more than 3,000; after two months only 1,500 effectives were left, and this at a time when the open breaches needed a force of at least 6,000 to defend them. After three months Verdier, commanding the besiegers, delcared in his elation that another fortnight would suffice to take the town. After four and a half months came the "Great Day of Gerona", when the French, in overwhelming force, assaulted four open breaches. Admittedly the weary, hungry soldiers of Ultonia[2] and Borbón should have been overrun but the whole town, businessmen, labourers, women and children flocked to the breaches and held fast against Napoleon's disciplined grenadiers. The priests abandoned their canonicals and banded themselves into eight companies of a *Cruzada gerundense* (Crusade of Gerona) battalion; a women's corps, the Company of Saint Barbara, was formed to carry away the wounded and bring munitions to the defences. But they did not limit themselves to these activities; General Saint-Cyr complained that "at every breath of air their ribbons were seen to float amidst the bayonets of the soldiers." Their commandant, Dona Lucía Fitz-gerard (or Fitzgerald), was not the only bearer of an Irish name; after four months of siege an "O'Donnel, issuing from the town, fell upon Souham's quarters, and obliged that general to fly in his shirt."[3] English were there too and at least one, called Marshal, partly atoned for the British cabinet's lethargy[4] by dying gallantly.

MARIANO ALVAREZ DE CASTRO was at once the inspiration of the bold and the dread of the faint-hearted. The small, spare, indefatigable figure with the wizened, parchment-like face was at first accepted with reserve by the regular troops he had come to command. This was in January 1809, after he had been superseded in Barcelona for disobeying orders to hand over the Castel of Montjuich which he commanded. There was no such interference in Gerona: he was nominally under the orders of Palacios, and Palacios held his position only subject to the approval of the tutelary St Narcissus, who was appointed generalissimo of the forces by sea and land, the ensigns of authority having, with due solemnity, been placed on his coffin. As he had been martyred in

The City walls of Gerona.

A.D. 306, the saint was still a comparative beginner, considerably junior to St James of Compostela, who had so often led the Spanish forces to victory.

When the siege began in May Alvarez de Castro issued the first of his famous manifestoes: "The death penalty for anyone, whatever his rank or condition, who has the vileness to suggest surrender or capitulation." Another proclamation was issued verbally while he was fighting in the front rank: "The second rank has orders to shoot without question those of us who take one step back." And when an officer enquired to what position he should withdraw in case he was repulsed, Alvarez suggested the cemetery. Wherever the fighting was fiercest the figure of Alvarez was seen, distinguished by the badge in his headgear: "For Ferdinand VII. Victory or Death." Ferdinand VII, the last and the worst of the male Bourbons. You have only to look at his portrait by Goya to realise for whom these gallant men and women were dying. By October, when Augereau took over command of the besiegers, the defenders were dying of hunger as well as wounds and medical supplies were exhausted. The French Marshal sent an envoy under flag of truce to offer an armistice of a month with free passage of supplies to the city. If at the end of that time had not arrived, the city was to surrender. Alvarez replied that in future emissaries would be fired on.

By autumn his malaria had recurred several times and he suffered the exhaustion and privations which were the common lot. Yet he forced himself to be present at every threatened point. In December, when the defenders were so weak that they could no longer stand, Alvarez roused himself from his sick bed for a last effort; by some magic his heroic spirit called forth one more drive and a general attack was made, during which captured ground and redoubts were retaken and the garrison of an outlying fort rescued. The next day, 7th December 1809, he became delirious and Extreme Unction was given. His deputy, Simón de Bolívar (not the liberator of South America) obtained fair terms of capitulation: such troops as could still walk were to march out with their arms and colours, food supplies were to be distributed immediately while looting and even billeting of the occupying forces was prohibited. So fell Gerona, after seven months of privation and heroism, the town of which Arthur Young wrote in 1787, "all this lacks upkeep and would not hold up an army for half an hour."[5] We do not know how many of the defenders died, but the siege claimed 15,000 French lives, or five times the number of the whole force of defending troops.

It is sad to have to record the fate of Alvarez. Too weak to march out with the survivors, he was taken to Figueras ten days later with a few faithful staff officers, under guard. Exhausted by interrogation, he was moved on Christmas Eve to Perpignan, where the filthy quarters assigned prompted him to ask with disdain, "Are these suitable quarters for a general, and is it you who pride yourselves on being soldiers?" Not unnaturally he fell ill again; then he was transferred to worse quarters, then to Narbonne, and finally back to the castle of Figueras. Here he died, and ugly rumours began to circulate, reinforced by the French burial party trying to help themselves to the dead hero's cloak.

Castanos, victor of Bailén, had the following inscription placed in the stables of the Castle of San Fernando in Figueras: "Here died of poison, on 22nd January 1810, victim of the iniquity of the tyrant of France, the Governor of Gerona Don Mariano Alvarez de Castro, whose heroic deeds will live for ever. In memory of his virtues His Excellency Senor Don Francisco Javier de Castaños, Captain-General of the Army of the Right, ordered this tablet to be placed 1815."

In 1823 Ferdinand VII, in whose name Alvarez had dedicated himself and his companions to death or victory, had repudiated every privilege that had been promised to his valiant, faithful people. Reforms were abolished, reformers killed and, to quell popular indignation, a French army under the Duke of Angoulême was called in to support the tyrant of Spain. On their way they destroyed the memorial to the man who had died in the service of the unspeakable Ferdinand.

It is customary in Spain for cities, as well as individuals, to be granted titles, a legacy of the Arabs. León, for instance, is "very noble, very loyal and illustrious"; there are the "illustrious, magnificent, noble, egregious, twice loyal and most excellent city of Valencia" and the "twice most noble, most faithful, twice notable, five times celebrated, head and pillar of all Catalonia, egregious and most excellent city of Barcelona". Gerona's title, since that siege, is short by contrast: it consists of only one word — IMMORTAL.

The siege of Zaragoza is better known, if only for the episode of AGUSTINA ZARAGOZA (yes, that was her first surname too) DOMÉNECH, immortalised in Byron's "Childe Harold". Through him the world got its picture of the indomitable maid, serving the cannon beside which her lover lay dead. The facts are different but detract in no way from her glory. She did, single-handed, serve a gun in a stricken battery, when a French storming column threatened to break through the defences. Her husband, a regular officer, was serving elsewhere; both were taken prisoner when Aragón was conquered by the French and both escaped when the column of captives reached the historic pilgrimage town of Puente la Reina. She became a legend in her own lifetime. Her escape was contrived by the common people who had heard of her heroism and she was officially appointed an officer in the Spanish army. Wellington received her in Cádiz and presented her with a pair of valuable, inlaid pistols which, after being fired, became miraculously armed with miniature bayonets. For a time her life seems to have been a trail of banquets and the persistent refusal of honours and rewards. She soon tired of this and made her way to besieged Tortosa where she commanded a battery and nobly sustained the reputation of the women of that city. Their fame dates from

1149, when Tortosa was besieged by the Almohads; so heroic were the women on this occasion that the Count of Barcelona conferred on them in a body the Order of the Axe, its red scarf and various privileges. One of these, observed into the present century, was that of walking ahead of the groom at their wedding. (The women of Beauvais in France have a similar privilege, won by a woman in the fifteenth century.) But the ancient heroism of Tortosa had declined and it was Agustina who fired the last shot when the inevitable surrender took place. For the second time she was a prisoner; again she gained her freedom and rejoined the Spanish forces, finishing her military career by fighting in the front line at the Battle of Vitoria. After the war she retired to a farm in Andalucïa and eventually died in Ceuta, being buried in a simple grave, distinguished only by the insignia of a Spanish officer. Throughout her life she probably saw nothing strange in the idea that women should fight like men.

And what, meantime, of the Girdle of Zobeida? About the year 1800, according to Dr Maranon a refugee French *marquise* sought support for a restoration of the old régime. Among her helpers was a certain Countess of Montijo, who contributed two enormous emeralds; we last heard of them in the possession of Don Juan of Austria. The fund was used to support the exiled Bourbons of France; the emeralds do not appear in any record until half a century later. Napoleon rose and fell; his nephew, Napoleon III, likewise rose and fell but enters this tale by marrying the daughter of the Countess of Montijo. One of his wedding presents to his beautiful bride was a pair of superb emeralds, which Eugenia used to wear as a pendant. They sustained their reputation for bringing bad luck; her husband died a few years after his "empire" collapsed at Sedan and Eugenia lived on in sorrow, mourning her only son and her lost beauty. I remember reading of her death in 1920 but no newspaper told us more than that her personal effects were bequeathed to her attendants; no one has discovered which of her ladies inherited the last jewels of Zobeida's fabulous girdle.

(left) Goya's famous portrait of Agustina Zaragosa. "Zaragosa" was her maiden name, which a Spanish woman uses even after marriage.

PART II
places

The Roman Aqueduct at Segovia.

CHAPTER NINE

The Roman Legacy: Tarragona

What follows is concerned chiefly with a review of visible and tangible evidence left by the various occupants of Spain; nevertheless, though in this chapter I deal mainly with the remains of what the Romans built, let us not lose sight of their far more important contributions: law, peace and communications. Without them Spain's later history would have been vastly different. Christianity, for example, at first a doctrine of peace and good will, could hardly have spread through a disorganised state or across waters infested by pirates; you have only to compare the speed of its diffusion inside and outside the empire. But most of us need something physical to transport us through time and Spain offers an abundance of remains. The thrill of digging up a Roman coin meant more to the novelist Pérez Galdós than did worldly success and the homage of learned societies.

One Roman town, Mérida, has its original bridge over half a mile long; the Roman drainage system is still in use and the original street plan can be reconstructed by reference to it. Another is Segovia, which you can visit on a day trip from Madrid. Its aqueduct, it is argued, is grander than France's famous Pont du Gard. Not only Roman bridges but also their aqueducts are usually attributed to a supernatural agency; such is the impact of technology on the artless. "The Devil's Bridge" is the usual name and before the Devil achieved popularity it was the high priest and the pope who took the title of *Pontifex Maximus* – Chief Bridge-builder. In Segovia the story is that a girl got tired of carrying water down to the valley and up to the town every day. She made the usual compact with the Devil – the shortage of souls in Hell seems to have passed, for we never hear of these compacts today – and the aqueduct was built overnight. Repenting of her bargain she went to the priest and the good man soon discovered that one stone was missing, so that the job was incomplete. By this display of sophistry virtue triumphed and the maiden had the best of it in both worlds. But it is often the smaller remains that leave the most vivid impression: an altar stone with the relief of a priest's *patera* and *prefericulum*[1] used as a building block in the church tower of Albarracín; a jointed, ivory doll in Tarragona Museum, found in the grave of a Roman child; the shape of a Roman amphora in daily use – these are the talismans that bring to life the people of long ago.

Tarragona is ideal for those who want to see what Rome could do for her subject territories, and incidentally to gain an impression of mediaeval Spain and, in particular, of Catalonia. If you walk along the broad *rambla* to the sea, a great statue faces you at the end of the boulevard: it is the Catalan admiral Roger de Lluria, who not only captured Malta and won the sea war against France and Provence in the thirteenth century, but also terrorised the coasts of the eastern Mediterranean so thoroughly that his name ranks high, even among pirates. He embodied the spirit and daring of the Catalans who, in the next generation, carved out a duchy for themselves in Greece. One episode is enough to project his character: when the King of France sued for a truce, Lluria sent a message that he would gladly continue the fight with a hundred galleys against France's three hundred and that he would not rest until "not a fish dares to show itself above water without the arms of Aragón on its scales." Behind the statue you stand on the Balcony of the Mediterranean. Far away to the right are the port and the quarter called the Barrio del Serrallo, though no one knows how it got its name. Was it a *seraglio* for some Moslem potentate, or was the word used as originally in popular Latin, when *serraculum* simply meant an enclosure, and as Evelyn used it when he wrote in Italy, "The Jews dwell as in a suburbe by themselves. I passed by the Piazza Judea, where their Seraglio begins"? There were many Jews in Tarragona and you can see a window sill in the town with a Hebrew inscription.

To your left is the delightful resort where Martial, the Spanish poet, wintered along with the cream of Roman society. Augustus, having inaugurated the campaign for the conquest of northern Spain, stayed here for the winter of 26 B.C.; from here he issued the edict that the doors of the Temple of Janus in Rome should be closed to signify that, for the first time in living memory, the whole Roman world was at peace. The district and its wines still deserve the eulogies of Roman writers who praised the *aprica litora*; the local hotels have improved since Aubry de la Motraye, in the seventeenth century, wrote that "the beds are veritable stores of fleas and other worse pests."[2] Casanova, on the other hand, voiced no complaints after spending the night here with Nina, official mistress of the Viceroy and Governor General of Catalonia. Perhaps she consoled him with the Spanish proverb which implies that sweethearts' beds need only be firm and level (*Cama de novio, dura y sin hoyo*).

If we walk to the left along the road overlooking the remains of the amphitheatre we are at the old town. Below us, in the centre of the amphitheatre, are the foundations of an early Christian basilica, presumably built on the site of the martyrdom of St Fructuoso and his deacons. Climbing the Avenida de al Victoria you see on your left the noble tower said to have been the governor's palace and hence still called the Praetorium, or alternatively the House of the Pilates, from the unreliable legends that Pontius Pilate was born here or was praetor of this part of Spain. It is, however, reasonable to accept the legend that later it was the residence of Visigothic kings and governors. From here onwards the golden walls of the Roman town are on your left, bathed in almost constant sunshine. The lower courses are Cyclopean – great unshaped blocks roughly fitted together without mortar – and represent the old Iberian town of the third century B.C. The lintels of the postern gates are especially noteworthy. What a mixture there is above! Roman squared blocks, mediaeval rubble, modern plaster that flakes away to reveal more Roman masonry. Houses are built into the wall and their wrought-iron balconies add to its charm. Tarragona is of course not the only Spanish city to preserve portions of its Roman wall, but hers are the most complete and best displayed. Astorga, León, Lugo, Coria, Barcelona and Gerona all show that they were once fortified by the legions.

At the top of the road the wall swings away to the left and you may enter the Archaeological Walk, strolling on gravel paths between lawn and shrub, cypress and pines, while you study the masonry of the old walls, no longer converted into dwellings. Stumps of columns rise from the grass, marble benches invite rest and meditation and old cannon point away over the plain to remind us that Tarragona was besieged and captured in the War of the Spanish Succession and, a hundred years later, by Napoleon. The guns probably saw service on both occasions. A laurel tree flourishes here and an inscription tells you that its parent grows on the Capitol, "the gift of Rome to her daughter city, whose name and deeds have always adorned her mother's fame." A little further, framed in cypresses, is a bronze replica of the famous marble statue of Augustus from Prima Porta, now in the Vatican Museum. It too was a present from the Italian Government, as was the bronze she-wolf suckling the twins Romulus and Remus, the Etruscan original being in the Capitoline Museum of Rome.

There are other Roman remains in the old city, inside the walls. There was a forum of course, and parts of it are still above ground, the more picturesque near the Plaza del Pallol, quite near the exit from the Archaeological Walk. Another forum has been discovered in the new town but is not really worth a visit. Paradoxically the dead are more living reminders. The large Roman and Palaeo-Christian Necropolis next to the tobacco factory has some mosaics and many, many empty sarcophagi. A fine specimen was used as a building-block over the right-hand entrance portal of the Cathedral. This is one of the finest in Europe, though it breaks no records for size, wealth, age or the number of workmen killed during its construction. It represents the era of transition between Romanesque and Gothic, thus avoiding the worst features of both. From the former it takes its solid appearance and some round arches, from the latter the impressive main portal, flanked by superlative statues and crowned by one of the largest rose windows in Europe – almost a record after all. Obviously you must get a guide, or at least a guide-book, if you want to study details. Here I am more interested in those aspects which illustrate the history I outlined, or even simply those I have grown to love.

In the first chapel on the right, the Baptistry, the font is a large Roman tank of marble popularly called "The Bath of Augustus"; those who have seen real Roman baths will disagree. Opposite, the first chapel on the left contains a replica of the famous Black

Column capitals. Entrance to the cloister at Tarragona Cathedral.

The Cloister of Tarrogona Cathedral.

Virgin of Montserrat and a retable by the famous Luis Borrassá, who introduced the international style of Gothic painting into Catalonia. It is worth asking to have the chapel lit up, for this is one of Tarragona's finest works of art. Another is the fifteenth-century alabaster retable of the high altar, lovingly studded with tiny carved details: a fly, a bee, a butterfly. At your right hand is a rare piece. It is the tomb of Archbishop Juan de Aragón who died in 1334 and who, smiling in his sleep, is immortalised in the Gothic style at its best. You will doubtless look with kindly tolerance at the relief of the angels bearing the soul of the departed to the Almighty – in a napkin. Or you may be lost in admiration at the masterly sculpture of the recumbent figure and the miniature saints waiting to welcome him to Heaven with the affection of old friends. My own favourite, however, is below the sarcophagus: each pedestal consists of a maned lion licking a cub and together they tell the illiterate their story with such simple sincerity that the six lines of Gothic script above are almost unnecessary. For the mediaeval Christian had been brought up on the *Speculum Ecclesiae*, the Mirror of the Church, by Honorius of Autun, and his symbolism goes back to the Bestiaries and through them to the *Physiologus*, believed to be a work of the second century. One of its beliefs was that the lioness brings forth lifeless cubs but that on the third day the father lion appears and licks the cubs, which instantly come to life. As a symbol of the Resurrection, portraying two days in the tomb and the rousing to eternal life through the Father's mediation, it ranks in mediaeval art with the same lesson told by Jonah's delivery from the belly of the whale. How suitably is it placed below the tomb, above which the Almighty is welcoming the soul of the departed!

The cloister is one of the cathedral's greater glories, where transition excels itself with groups of three rounded Romanesque arches collected under pointed Gothic ones and surmounted by pairs of pierced stone lights in Arab style, the incorporation of the cross in some compatible with *Mudéjar* workmanship. The entrance is through a fine divided Romanesque arch whose carvings, like all the best of this epoch, are attractive in their naïvety. How would the rude, unlettered Christian know that the angel was bringing a message to the three kings, if they did not go to bed with their crowns on? Or realise that the Roman soldiers guarding the Saviour's tomb would not be dressed in contemporary armour?

In the west wall is a marble *mihrab* with a carved inscription that provides yet another mystery. This recess, which is supposed to indicate the side of the mosque that points to Mecca, is said by most writers to have been brought from elsewhere as a trophy. They believed too implicitly the statement that Tarragona was an abomination of desolation for four centuries; Gudiol, it is true, discusses the hypothesis of a "supposed" Arab mosque in Tarragona, but votes for importation. Yet I cannot conceive of a town under the rule of a Moslem *wali* and garrison that did not

Detail of a bas-relief at the Cathedral of Tarragona.

have a mosque. You may judge my delight when I found the following in Condé's much maligned book: "It was during the year of 349 [Arab calendar of course] that Abderahman Anasir caused to be constructed at Tarragona the *mihrab*, or interior oratory of the principal mosque; over the grand arch of the façade the following inscription was engraved in the most precious marble that could be procured."[3] Here follows a precise rendering of the invocation which is still legible: "In the name of Allah. May the blessings of God fall on Abd al-Rahman, Prince of the Faithful, whose life may God preserve, who ordered this work to be done by the hands of Giafar, servant of his household, in the year nine and forty and three hundred." The equivalent in our reckoning is A.D. 960, so that God preserved the life of Abderrahman III for one year more. To the statement that the Moslem frontier was withdrawn to the Ebro before his reign I would reply that records exist of repairs being made to the aqueduct of Tarragona on the instructions of Abderrahman III.

A favourite showpiece in the cloister is the abacus crowning twin columns, on which is carved the Procession of the Rats. On the left you see them carrying the "corpse" of a cat to its grave, and on the right the cat has come to life and is claiming its stupid victims. This may be based on a Spanish proverb which says, "The mouse is wise but the cat is wiser" (*Mucho sabe el rato, pero más el gato*). Street admired the carving as an example of humour but I suspect that it was made in all seriousness to convey to the monks that the Enemy is most to be feared when apparently subdued. There are many other examples of the same theme, in Tarragona and other Western churches, a variation on the primitive fable of the beast of prey shamming dead which is known from Upper Egypt to the Amazon.

In the Chapel of Corpus Christi, which opens off the cloister, is the dark, fourteenth-century retable of St Bartholomew which Street saw in a transept. ". . . I deciphered, among other things," he wrote, "the diverting history of a child who wouldn't grow up. In twenty-five years he wore out four nurses, who lie dead about the floor."[4] He is referring to the middle panel on the right and the dead wet-nurses (their occupation prominently stressed by the artist) lie under the bed, arranged like sardines. The whole retable seems to be an account of a forgotten miracle, for St Bartholomew is shown entering the room, prepared to exorcise the demon; the "baby", in face, is a miniature devil, horns and all. Some will feel a breath of prophecy in the retable: Charles II of Spain, last of the Hapsburgs, was not weaned until he was five and during this time used up fourteen wet-nurses.

Of the many treasures in this Cathedral — and Street finished his account with the hope that he might return to see more — I shall mention only a few: there is the exquisitely painted *artesonado* in the Sacristy; the Roman wall with evidence of a later Visigothic church that forms one side of the chapter-house; the tapestries that Augustus Hare described as hanging in the body of the Cathedral and which are now displayed in the Diocesan Museum. They are said to have been bought in London at the sale of church furniture after the dissolution of the monasteries by Henry VIII, and may once have hung in St Paul's Cathedral. In the overgrown cemetery behind the Cathedral is the Chapel of St Thecla which, for tradition is strong here, contains elements reminding one of a Roman temple. The same tendency is even more marked in a chapel inside one of the courtyards of the seminary across the road; it stands on rock, marking the highest point of the hill of Tarragona, and is said to have been built on the site where St Paul preached. Don't be surprised; lots of people don't know that he preached here, in fact only the Tarragonese really know it. As you can see, it is a pretty chapel, with the Roman temple façade strongly stressed, and at first sight you feel inclined to ignore the experts' opinion that it is mediaeval. Then you look at the under-surface of the lintel and find that it is a Visigothic door jamb put to a new use. You can't explain that away. All this may make you keen to see Tarragona for yourself. If you do, look for the ghost of the ancient hospital in the house fronts facing the south side of the Cathedral; the window opening

The chapel of San Pablo in Tarragona.

in the street called Escribanías Viejas, made of a Hebrew tombstone resting across two inscribed Roman tablets; a mediaeval arcade running the length of a street, the ancient doorways, the venerable courtyards.

If you have time, and especially if you have not been able to visit Segovia, take the Lérida road and pull into the side after three kilometres. A short walk through a wood takes you to the Tarragona aqueduct which, as late as the last century, was still bringing water to the town from twenty miles away. As usual, it is called "The Devil's Bridge". There is another Devil's Bridge in Catalonia, across the Llobregat at Martorell. It is probably Carthaginian and was later restored by the Romans. Its legend differs from that of Segovia, for at Martorell the Iberians were fighting a rearguard action against the Romans in the second century B.C. They found the river at their back and, to save his men, their leader sold his soul to the Devil in return for the bridge, which was duly constructed overnight. You will note that in these tales it is the Devil who keeps his side of the bargain. The only point of interest in the story is that the Devil came to Spain two centuries before God.

The Tower of Santa María de Illescas, a fine example of Mudéjar architecture.

CHAPTER TEN

Islamic Survivals

It would be too much to expect that an occupation of eight centuries should leave evidence of only one culture. Remains of the Omayyad period, from A.D. 756 to about 1030, show the influence of Persian, Syrian, Coptic and Mesopotamian art. The forest of columns in the Great Mosque of Córdoba is often adduced as a sign that the builders were desert dwellers who treasured a dream of shady groves, and there are other examples of contemporary art and architecture which have the same mythical origin. I have made it clear that the Arabs who first came to Spain – and their Berber troops too who are also included here – were not desert nomads.

When the Caliphate went down it was followed by the *taifas*, where ostentation was combined with a love of learning and beauty. Then came the Almoravids and after them the Almohads; with them Spain had its first taste of desert fanatics. But only for a while. In the langorous surroundings of the *taifa* courts that they overthrew, austerity did not hold out for long and the desert dynasties duly went through the same stages of internal disorder and gracious living as had their predecessors. One reads how these Moroccan tribesmen showed their fanatical hostility to art, literature and free speculation in the realm of thought. But it was precisely during the time of Berber hegemony (1056–1269) that geography was enriched by al-Bakri and al-Idrisi, Medicine by Ibn Zuhr (better known today as Avenzoar), Philosophy by Ibn Bajja (Avempace), Abu'l Walid Ibn Rushd (Averroes) and Ibn Tufayl;

and the long dynasty of Spanish mystics — Saint Teresa, Saint John of the Cross, even Ignatius Loyola — was inaugurated by the Murcian Ibn al-Arabí. And perhaps their greatest contribution to civilisation was through their intolerance and the expulsion of Mozarabs and Jews. Those who found refuge in the Christian lands to the north brought their skills with them.

That is why the only complete Mozarab churches that remain today are in the territory of the early Reconquest. See, for instance, the Church of San Miguel de Escalada near León. Admittedly it was built by Mozarab refugees of an earlier epoch when, under the Caliphate, an epidemic of martyrdom threatened to wipe out the subject Christians, but it is as good an example as we shall find. Mozarabic art is picturesque and the last word has not yet been said about its provenance. The rounded horseshoe arch, for instance: is it the successor of their Visigothic forbears, jealously preserved through centuries of servitude? Is it the Islamic arch that we have seen at Córdoba, itself the descendant of the Visigothic arch? Or is it the Sassanid arch of the Persians?

It is as well to realise that a better appreciation of the period and the achievements of the Moslems can be gained from museums than from surviving buildings. I concede that museums may be dull; that of course depends on how little knowledge you have when you enter and how much when you leave. With only a superficial idea of the chief events of Spanish history, such as is compressed into the first part of this book, eyes may well be opened when they see the treasures of the minor arts displayed. Nevertheless the finest monument of the Caliphate and the earlier emirate is afforded by the great Mosque-Cathedral of Córdoba.

Few guides draw attention to the following features in this impressive building, with its forest of columns, its infinite vistas of striped horseshoe arches and its solemn gloom, no longer relieved by the light of thousands of oil lamps. First, when you stand before the ornate mosaic *mihrab*, or prayer niche that is meant to show the direction of Mecca, look above and note the ribs of the cupola. These are arranged in four pairs and where they cross they leave an octagonal figure which serves as the base on which a small dome rests. Its importance lies in its date: built before the year 1000 it is far older than the oldest ribbed ceiling of any existing church and there is little doubt that the builders of the Christian West got their inspiration here. Then note the mosaics that cover the inside of the cupola and especially the curved, lustred bricks of the supporting rim, adorned with tile patterns in green and manganese brown. They look as fresh today as when they were set in place in A.D. 965. Next, study the *mihrab* itself. The gorgeous mosaics are Byzantine in style and origin, even though they bear Arabic texts. They were placed there by Byzantine artists lent for the occasion by the Emperor Nicephoros Phocas. If you want to see how the Moslems made mosaics you have only to look at the Capilla Real and see the much later dado made by using pieces of coloured tile instead of shiny cubes. This form of Islamic decoration is one of the few that persisted throughout.

Again, compare the scheme of decoration of the Capilla Real (sometimes confused with the neighbouring chapel, the Villa-viciosa) with the rest of the mosque. The latter, with the exception of the later Christian Cathedral in the centre, is all earlier than the year 1000; the Capilla Real is the work of Moslems living in Córdoba after the city was reconquered. Once you have passed the stage of awe that the mosque inspires you will have no difficulty in appreciating the essential differences between the florid, over-decorated work of the *Mudéjares* and the simple monumental concept of the emirs and caliphs. It is the same difference that distinguishes the interior of the church of Paray-le-Monial from the fripperies of the age of Louis XV. It is worth noting, for it forms the basis of many of the distinctive features of later Spanish art.

Another interesting feature, this time on the outside walls, is the style of merlon (the uprights between the embrasures). Their stepped design is so striking that they were copied on tile friezes for centuries and are still reproduced as "battlements" on villas that are the counterpart of twentieth century "pseudo-Tudor" in England. The origin of the stepped merlon goes back to Achaemenid Persia and it may still be seen among the ruins of Persepolis, dating from five centuries before Christ. In the form I have illustrated they also survive on the tenth-century Cairo mosque of al-Azhar. In fact, the further you delve into Islamic art, the more often you will find its features spread over vast areas, still reproducing Indian, Persian or Byzantine characters. It is far more difficult to see what isn't there then what is; the statement is especially true if what isn't there ought to be there. In this case you have to be reminded that nowhere in the Great Mosque is there an example of the elaborate caliphal column capital. They were hand-carved by the thousand in the royal workshops at Medina Azzahra a few miles from Córdoba; some are being replaced during the elaborate reconstruction of that fairy palace. After the fall of the Caliphate they were sold throughout Spain and North Africa and still turn up in the strangest places.

Of the minor arts, there are enough examples to support the claim that many European industries had their origin in Spanish manufacture. One which is peculiar to the period of the caliphate is the ivory casket, examples of which can be seen in museums in many countries. Delicately carved, and often carrying an inscription in Cufic characters, giving the names of the donor, recipient and maker, they were used by Moslem women as jewel- or cosmetic-boxes. When they fell into the hands of conquering Christians they were so highly esteemed that they were used for

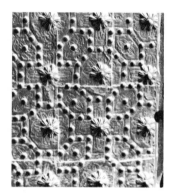

A church door at Daroca.

A caliphal column capital.

the preservation of holy relics, and thanks to this unforeseen use they have survived for a thousand years.

Among other industries leather-work, lustre ware and woven silk must be mentioned, but the introduction of paper, an essential preliminary to the invention of printing, was probably of more consequence. Spanish Moslems, both before and after the Christian Reconquest, produced many eastern fabrics that survive today: *bougran* was the buckram of Bokhara; *zatony* was satin, and *sarga* is today known as serge. And the Spanish language, which inherited and handed on these terms, kept for itself some hundreds of Arabic words which are still in daily use. The introduction of paper illustrates the fact that the Arabs were transmitters rather than inventors; they learned how to make paper from Chinese artisans when they captured Samarkand in 704, and from there the knowledge was diffused throughout the world of Islam. Lustre ware soon became popular throughout Europe and was imitated in Italy, where it was given the name *majolica*. This does not imply that Mallorca was a centre for the industry, which seems to have been located on the mainland, from Almeria to Valencia; the name derives from the fact that pottery was carried to Italy in Mallorcan ships. There is, however, another theory based on the fact that there was a pottery at Inca, in Mallorca. The civic coat-of-arms of Inca displays a greyhound; this was a frequent subject for decoration on pottery from Valencia, so the Italians wrongly ascribed it all to Mallorca. The use of lustre tiles for roofing is also typical of this area.

The few pieces of decorated wood that survive from the first period, such as those discovered in the ceiling of Córdoba Mosque, show that elaborate ornamentation was practised early. It reached a peak much later and, as we shall see, persisted under Christian rule. Decorative metal work antedates the Moslems but they beautified it and handed on their skill, so that it was still in evidence during the Middle Ages. See, for instance, a church door at Daroca.

From the same period a few castles survive, usually only as shells. Some of those which were built along the south coast — Marbella for instance — to face the threat of the Egyptian Fatimids were converted to their own use by the *taifa* kings and, later, the Christian reconquerors. Other castles were built on the northern frontier of al-Andalus in an attempt to check the steady advance of the Leonese and Castilians. A good example is the castle of Gormaz, a magnificent ruin guarding a bridge over the Duero near Soria. Built by the Caliphs and taken from the Moslems by Alfonso VI, it was given to the Cid to mark the end of one of their estrangements.

The next epoch to leave distinctive remains is that of the Almohades (roughly A.D. 1150–1220). Their two most typical productions were the double wall, part of one of them surviving at the northern boundary of Seville, and the decorated minarets that can still be seen in the south of Spain and Morocco. Panels of *sebka* work are the principal feature of these square towers; *shabka* is Arabic for a net and the pattern is indeed a network of wavy lines, often produced by projecting brick courses. The best example is the Giralda of Seville.

The last purely Islamic style I want to mention is that of the Nasrids in Granada. The Alhambra Palace is the most complete, the best restored and the most popular monument of Islamic art that survives. Its elegant, slender columns, mosaic tiles, ornamental stucco and honeycomb ceilings have delighted millions of visitors. Here decoration reaches such a peak of variety and intricacy that it is often spoken of as decadent, or "rócoco". It may be so, but it is still oriental and, as Sordo says, "In Western art, decoration is used to ennoble an already coherent structure . . . In Eastern art, decoration is used for its own sake, for ostentation or . . . to conceal the poverty of a few mud walls."[1] Those of the Alhambra, while by no means humble, certainly give no hint of the richness that awaits you behind them. They are simply another example of the Oriental's tendency to look inwards and to arrange his home life round an interior patio, with the greatest emphasis on privacy.

Nasrid art may also be seen in the royal palace of Seville, the Alcázar, built partly by artisans lent to Pedro the Cruel by his friend Mohamed V, King of Granada. Note especially the height of complexity obtained in the geometric patterns. The ceilings are all in *alfarje*, designs made by strips of larch and an inlay of ivory or differently coloured woods, as well as painting and appliqué. The work is usually called *artesonado* but the term is properly applied only to such ceilings as have the shape of an inverted trough. Corners and dome supports are a riot of honeycomb niches of painted plaster and of stalactites made in the same way. When ceilings of such opulence crown walls whose stucco is carved into endless flower patterns and yards of poems and invocations in decorative Arabic script, over tile mosaic dadoes whose colours have kept their freshness for six centuries, the visitor is seeing the supreme example of an art unique in its exuberance and preservation.

Like so much that was originally Roman, irrigation was adapted and improved by the Arabs. Much of the agricultural produce in the south and east still depends on its efficient working and in many places Arab aqueducts and water-wheels still function. In Valencia the weekly meeting of the Water Board hears complaints in public, outside the Door of the Apostles of the Cathedral; in a democratic way, decisions are given by an elected committee that dispenses with written records. The Board dates back to at least the tenth century and still meets on Thursdays, the day before the Moslems' sabbath.

Mudéjar has been termed the only truly Spanish style. It is certainly a style in its own right and not merely the grafting of Islamic decoration on a Romanesque or Gothic structure. It may be regarded as akin to a musical composition, the creating of thematic material and its constructive treatment.[2] The outstanding features of Aragonese *mudéjar*, as we shall see it at Teruel, are the complex decoration and the skilful blending of brick, wood, plaster and ceramic in a highly original manner. Elsewhere it adopts a hundred expedients to preserve its oriental flavour, even to the carving of an Arabic text – "There is no God but Allah" – over a church door. In the cloister of Tarazona (not Tarragona) Cathedral, in the province of Zaragoza, you can see superb stone lacework made by *mudéjares*. The custom of keeping subject people as workers, with little impediment to the practice of their own religion, was introduced by the Moslems. The Christians did not adopt it until Alfonso VI found himself lord of a host of skilled artisans when he captured Toledo in 1085. From this date we can speak of *mudéjar* art. The first major work that I know is the cloister of San Juan de Duero, at Soria. The interlacing arches are one of Islam's first contributions to Western decoration; we saw it on the facade of Toledo's San Cristo de la Luz and this example was built for the Knights of St John about 200 years later. The façades of many early English cathedrals, carrying the same interlacing arcade, were therefore built before

The Tower of San Martín in Teruel.

The cloister of Tarrazona Cathedral.

Teruel Cathedral.

The Polygonal Tower, Teruel.

the Soria example, but we must remember that oriental influence had spread through Europe, from both Spain and Sicily, before the Norman conquest.

Carpentry, too, was at one time almost entirely in the hands of *mudéjares*. To them we owe, not only a great number of intricately decorated ceilings, but the great chest in the museum of León Cathedral and the organ casing in the Old Cathedral of Salamanca. Ornamented bureaux or *barguenos* were another speciality that the *mudéjares* made in their workshops at Vargas (whence the name) near Toledo. The geometric patterns and the general form of construction persist to this day. The Moslems, in fact, handed on their skills to those Christians who were interested in learning; in Seville the art of carpentry was so highly regarded that its practitioners were registered in four specialities, of which one was again subdivided into *lazeros, non-lazeros* and *jumétricos* (geometricos). The first two dealt with the presence or absence of radiating figures with eight, twelve or more points, made of lines that cross again and again and never seem to end. In 1633 a full account of one style of carpentry was published in Seville by Diego Lopes de Arenas; although he was a Christian (and in any case Moslems were not tolerated at that time) his work is so full of Arabic terms that it is not properly understood today.

Islamic influence persisted long after the expulsion of the *moriscos* (converted Moslems) in 1609. Even the Arabic language was spoken openly until officially prohibited a few years later. And yet, later still, it was possible for a knife to be manufactured with an Arabic inscription on one face of the blade, "With the help of God I will inflict death upon thy adversary," and on the other, "Knife factory of Antonio González. Albacete, 1705." Arabic script, in fact, has strangely penetrating powers, even when not understood. This may be partly due to its artistic appeal, whether the Cufic or Naskhi characters are used; thus many mediaeval Christian carvings and embroideries had a "mock" Cufic strip at the margins. Even the celebrated "Coronation of the Virgin" by Fra Lippo Lippi, in the Uffizi Gallery of Florence, shows an attempt at Arabic script on the border of the Virgin's scarf.

Among the lesser known but more impressive *mudéjar* works are the great castles of La Mota and Coca in Castile. Made chiefly of brick, they are so massive and yet so elegant that they remain in the memory when much else has been forgotten. The Castle of Coca is indeed so fairy-like, for all its strength, that it was used for the making of the film, "Camelot". Apart from these, a host of other *mudéjar* works can be seen in many parts of Spain and the infinite variations through which the craft of ceramics developed in itself provides sufficient material for a book.

When we come to Teruel in Lower Aragón we find the happiest blend of Eastern and Western art.[3] Here at last we have ornamentation on a structure worthy of it. This is *mudéjar* at its best, and serves to bring home another truth. The style has for centuries been regarded as the product of subject people in the service of Christian masters. This is to confuse the aesthetic with the ethnic and to quote Guastavino, "A style is defined by its own character and not by its artisans ... Let us not forget that, however truly the art called *mudéjar* began and developed at the hands of the Moslem artisans of the Christian kingdoms, it does not remain as the exclusive inheritance of that social class, but is also produced by non-Moslem hands and persists through times when *mudéjar* no longer existed in Spain, spreading even to Spanish America." I would go further and remind the reader that the proportion of Arab and Moorish blood in many of the Moslems was negligible; the distinction, therefore, is not even ethnic, merely religious. Who knows what blood, Iberian, Roman, Gothic, Vandal, Berber, Kabyle, Jewish or Arabic, ran in the veins of the men, women and even children who delighted in building the gorgeous towers that still enthral us in Teruel? Even the concept of a quasi-servile population needs revision. For centuries after the capture of Teruel by Alfonso II of Aragón in 1171, Moslem inhabitants and Christian conquerors lived together in peace and concord. The former were protected by special laws and even their industry was safeguarded, so that the prices of "pots, pitchers and other vessels" were fixed by law as early as 1176. Tolerance and harmony persisted for nearly three centuries and bequeathed us the masterpieces we can still admire. Then, in 1412, Saint Vincent Ferrer visited the town and was shocked by the excessive liberty enjoyed by Moslem and Jew. A revivalist in the good old tradition of Peter the Hermit, he preached conversion, pointed out the road to salvation and hounded to death those who were too obstinate to profit by his words. A strange contradiction,

The Castle de la Mota.

equally at home as counsellor and confessor in Avignon to the Spanish Antipope Benedict XIII or leading his ragged penitents from town to town, whipping up their passions with his matchless oratory, fervent and austere, distilling intolerance and hatred with the fire of his fanaticism.

Teruel has the grandest and most profuse of all *mudéjar* works. The tower of San Martín, just inside the Andaquilla gate, may be taken as a fair example. Like other converted watch-towers, it straddles a street and is crowned with battlements. Only the sightseer who falls under the spell of this superb edifice will take the trouble to study its ornamental detail with field-glasses: he will be repaid by seeing a fascinating variety of patterns in brickwork, some modelled on the maze of laths that criss-cross an *artesonado* ceiling, others forming complicated interwoven blind arcades or chevrons. Then, to relieve the pale gold or rosy glow of brickwork,

The tiled roofs of Villajoyosa in Valencia.

the eye travels over ceramic colonnettes, discs, stars, diamonds or chequers, in green, white, turquoise, tangerine or purple.

A walk round the city may help us to understand how three religions co-existed in amity. On the east side the once forbidding walls have a friendly air, helped by windows, balconies, trees and a loggia. They were not always so welcoming. In 1484 two inquisitors were sent here to set up a branch agency of the Holy Office. A large proportion of the inhabitants consisted of *conversos* and practising Jews and it was chiefly the former, who had most to fear from the Inquisition, who influenced the authorities to refuse admission to the inquisitors. It was an easy matter to excommunicate the city's inhabitants, as bishops were at this time empowered to do; the Pope, however, thought otherwise and, possibly resenting the fact that the profits of the Spanish Inquisition remained in Spain, annulled the excommunication.

King Ferdinand the Catholic now intervened with armed force. The city submitted in the spring of 1485 and the following year such Jews as had not anticipated the inevitable by emigrating were massacred. With the departure of those who, in the words of Santiago Sebastián, had given vitality to the city since the thirteenth century, Teruel fell into decay. Still on the east side, in the line of the fortifications, stands the unique polygonal tower on the site of the original Moorish *alcázar*. Now shorn of its battlements and partly converted, with a tiny penthouse peeping at the rising sun, the Torreón de Ambeles still represents an aesthetically satisfying experiment in military architecture. The walk, with the city on your left and an impressive view on your right, is spoiled by the heavy traffic which assails your ears and nose. Nevertheless you should go on until you have seen the aqueduct built in the sixteenth century by the French engineer Vedel, the memory of whose genius is kept alive by at least two other masterpieces in this part of Spain.

But back to the Pride of Teruel. There are four magnificent *mudéjar* towers, two basically Romanesque, the others Gothic, and all with the richest decoration. In a vague way they remind you of the four-square Giralda of Seville, and it is difficult to decide whether they are nearer to minarets or bell towers. They should rate among Spain's greatest glories. The Cathedral has one, of course, and its lantern also shows the features of Aragonese *mudéjar* building. Its history, too, is typically Spanish. The interior has undergone at least five renovations, the most important being in the thirteenth and fourteenth centuries. About this time a Gothic-*mudéjar* plan was carried out by Juzaff, a Moor from Zaragoza, assisted by his co-religionists Zalema, Ali, Abraim and Mahomat, while a Christian painter, Domingo Peñaflor, decorated the ribbing, the necessary funds being lent by the Jewish community of Teruel. The Inquisition, Saint Vincent Ferrer, pogroms and forcible mass conversions of Moslems were still in the distant, undreamt of future. So was the civil war of 1936–9, during which Teruel was in the front line and sadly damaged, though most of the harm has been made good by skilful restoration. An unexpected consequence was the unmasking of an early *artesonado* ceiling in the nave. Shaped like an inverted trough and partitioned by the intricate geometric meanderings of the laths, it shows a wealth of painted panels from the brushes of anonymous artists. The style is somewhat naïve and has its own appeal: kings and queens, priests and Moors, knights and dragons live and talk and fight in simple, brilliant colours, an unequalled record of early Gothic painting. The geometric friezes, some decorated with mock-Cufic figures, remind us of the happy days when races and religions could unite for their mutual advantage and the greater glory of God.

The Church of San Miguel at Guadalajara which contains the tomb of Alvar Hañez, the Cid's second in command.

Santa María del Naranco at Oviedo.

CHAPTER ELEVEN

Traces of the Visigoths

The Visigothic bequest to Spain was not a great one and even St Isidore's learned contributions were in the Christian-Latin tradition. Little of their language survives in modern Spanish; the two hundred or so words of Germanic origin are said to deal mostly with war or clothing. Their nobility were called *ricos hombres*, a term that persisted for a thousand years. Though this could be translated today as "rich men", the stem *ric-* appears in all Indo-European languages to signify "powerful" or "noble" and crops up, from *rajah* to *rex*, with the meaning of power rather than wealth. By Germanic custom the king governed with the advice and consent of these great men; much later, as feudal barons, they were to vex the kings of England, France and Spain. Their *hombres buenos*, or good men, are a still more interesting survival. Their status appears to have been much like that of the "twelve good men and true" who figure as jurymen from Anglo-Saxon times and they appear in the chronicles now as assessors, now as counsellors. *Hombres buenos* are still used in Spanish civil law and certain classes of litigation are not accepted by the courts of law until a settlement has been attempted by "good men" selected by the litigants from among private individuals. These are, of course, only survivals; tribal law soon gave way largely to Roman law, if only because a Latin language was adopted by the Visigoths within two generations.

Still stranger survivals exist from the "good men" of mediaeval Spain. One of the oldest families is that of the dukes of Medina

Sidonia. The full name of the man who commanded the Spanish Armada was Alonso Pérez de Guzmán el Bueno, descended from the Guzmán we met in Chapter 1, who, rather than betray his trust allowed his son to be killed. His reward was the title "El Bueno", the Good, added to the family name. Now "Guzmán" is itself a survival of the Gothic *Guth Man*, so that the family name now reads "Good Man the Good".

Tangible Visigothic remains are encountered in many parts of Spain. Tombs have been found be the hundred, often grouped round the chancel of a church and hence as close as possible to a holy relic. From such cemeteries many small articles of dress and ornament have been recovered, useful in the study of the minor arts. Baptisteries and churches may be found in various parts of the country, usually off the beaten track but well worth a visit; I especially recommend the beautiful little church of San Pedro de la Nave, near Zamora. These churches, mostly built in the seventh century, have some charming features and incorporate decorative work of varying origin. First, the buildings are small; secondly, there is a strong resemblance between some of their patterns of decoration, such as wheels and stylised flowers, and the carved motifs seen on many Hispano-Roman tombstones; thirdly, there is such obvious borrowing of Byzantine themes that some authors simply class all Visigothic remains as Byzantine. Of course there was close contact between the Visigoths and the Roman empires in Thrace, again in Italy, and once more during the eighty years' Byzantine occupation of Southern Spain, but that is no reason for withholding credit for their artistic achievements. Another source of external influence is sixth-century Italy, possibly commemorating the short period when Theodoric, the enlightened Ostrogothic king, assumed the regency of Spain. But under and behind these more obvious and largely decorative contributions can be found a debased classical model, copied from Roman buildings.

The horseshoe arch seen in all Visigothic churches is *not* derived from the Moorish; on the contrary, it is likely that the Moslems adopted it from Spain, where it had arrived, originally from the East, through Roman agency. Items common to Visigothic and Byzantine decoration are the rosette and the "vine meander", a kind of endless rope that twines on itself and sprouts vine leaves at every turn. This and another typical feature of Visigothic decoration, the horizontal arrangement of a single frieze, are seen clearly on the Chapel of Santa María de Quintanilla de las Viñas, near Burgos,

Other architectural and sculptural reminders of their age can be seen in the churches of San Juan de Baños (Palencia) and Santa Combe de Banda (Orense); we shall return to the former. But many feel that it was in the minor arts that the Visigoths excelled. Belt clasps, brooches, buckles, all worked in bronze or precious metal and inset with stones or coloured glass, are richly barbaric; a list of the valuables carted off by the first Moslem invaders gives one an idea of the wealth and splendour of court and church. Seeing them in a museum showcase you may be struck by their resemblance to earlier styles; St Isidore, indeed, described the persistence of the Roman *Inaures* (earrings), *Torques* (collars) and *Fibulae* (brooches) among the Visigoths. The fabulous treasure of Guarrazar (Toledo) was largely smuggled out of Spain before its discovery was reported. Nine of the precious gold, jewelled votive crowns can be seen in the Cluny Museum in Paris, but a minority were kept where they belong and should be seen in Madrid. A replica of one hangs in the church at Venta de Baños, The name means "baths" and the remains of a Roman spa are hard by the church of San Juan, which was built by King Recceswinth as a thank-offering for being cured of the stone. The builders helped themselves to Roman columns which were found in the baths, where you can see two horseshoe arches, identical with those of the church, dating from a Visigothic restoration.

Although I write of "Visigothic art", there is no certainty that any member of that ruling caste could turn his hand to this or any other kind of manual task. It is, however, suggestive that a Visigothic refugee, Theodulf, built an oratory at Saint-Germigny des Prés (Loiret, France), which showed the characteristic features of Spanish Visigothic architecture and decoration. But this was long after the fall of Roderick's kingdom and it may well be that some to the Gothic aristocracy had to give up their taboos and become craftsmen. Among surviving prohibitions in Richard Ford's day was riding on assback, "a disgrace and degradation to the Gothic hidalgo"; and when poor, deluded Don Quixote had been so badly beaten by the muleteers that he could no longer mount his Rocinante and the friendly labourer was bringing him home on his own donkey, "he waited till it was rather darker, so that no one should see the battered gentleman on so shameful a

The Church of San
Juan de Baños.

mount."[1] So shameful, indeed, that it was the last insult
reserved for condemned prisoners, who were taken to the scaffold
seated backwards on a donkey.

The last and perhaps most significant bequest of the Goths was
an aristocratic aloofness which went with a fanatical pride in
purity of blood, that Germanic myth which crops up every now
and then. On this was based the social scale of grandee, hidalgo
and caballero and the proud boast of such families was their *sangre
castiza*, their clean blood untainted by the black fluid which
served to convey oxygen and nutriment to the tissues of Jew or
Moslem. As elsewhere, this was a myth in Spain too, for
intermarriage with these races was so common that by the end of
the Middle Ages hardly a family existed without this "taint" in its
pedigree.

Spain preserves written records from all her invaders. Thus
Roman tombstones are plentiful in museums and even as
building-blocks in old towns. A brick from Itálica (Seville) bears
the first two lines of Virgil's *Aeneid* in the same first-century
cursive script that we see at Pompeii. The Visigoths, imitating all
that was Roman, based their tombstones on the old model, finding
the slate of north-western Spain especially useful. Parchments
covering the whole period of Visigothic rule are found, not only in
the archives, but in the museums of Spain, Britain, France,
Germany and the Vatican. The first example of colour illustration
is found in the Ashburnham Pentateuch in the Bibliothèque
Nationale in Paris; most authorities now consider that it is
Spanish, dating from the days of St Isidore. If they are right, then

the primitive, crude miniatures of the tenth and eleventh centuries are not to be viewed as early striving for artistic expression, but as degenerate remains of what was once a flourishing and sophisticated art form.

A study of Mozarabic art fills gaps in our knowledge. In the remote monastery of Liébana a monk named Beatus compiled an illustrated commentary on the Books of Revelations and Daniel. He used the current art forms brought from al-Andalus by refugee Mozarabs; the existing copies, wherever they are found, all show the characteristic horseshoe arches, parallel folds of clothing and certain peculiarities of human features. These are freely accepted as Visigothic in origin. Quite often a Visigothic scene from an illuminated manuscript is repeated in the Beatus as well as in certain carved column capitals, for instance at San Pedro de la Nave (Zamora). The ultimate source is said to be early Coptic art in Egypt, from where ideas travelled along North Africa to Spain. A bold but erudite student has even given the date of the arrival of the style of miniatures in Visigothic Spain as the seventh century. This would allow their inclusion in the works of St Isidore, who was writing until A.D. 636. Matilde López Serrano has proposed a

Column capital at Santa Cristina de Lena.

A Visigothic chancel screen at Santa Cristina de Lena.

touchstone by which this branch of art, in both book illustrations and carvings, can be recognised: it is the presence of a characteristic frame round each subject, as though to define a picture.

Though it is convenient to refer to a "Mozarabic art" the term means no more than the end result of borrowing from Visigothic, caliphal, Byzantine and hence ultimately Roman and oriental models. So great was the unrest of the times and so widespread the movement of populations that a mixture of styles was inevitable; the Mozarabic is fortunate in being a harmonious blend and therefore artistically acceptable. One of its best examples is the Church of San Miguel de Escalada, south of León. Here, in true Mozarabic style, not only are the arches reminiscent of the Visigothic horseshoe, but the ground plan of the apse is likewise that of a horseshoe.

The Spaniards in the north, who remained unconquered by the Moslems, developed their own styles in art. Those of the Pyrenees will have to be passed over here in favour of the early buildings of the Asturias; these survive in and around Oviedo, which became the capital of Asturian resistance about the year 800, under Alfonso II (the Chaste). An interesting question now arises: Asturian documents of the ninth century have been preserved in the Escorial and in these it is stressed that the Asturian dynasty is a continuation of the Visigothic kingdom. Why then, we ask, do these early Asturian churches differ in so many essentials from surviving Visigothic churches? It is a question which admits of various answers; but is noteworthy that the legend of Visigothic parentage began only during the reign of Alfonso III (866–910), for his early records make no mention of it. It may perhaps be regarded as an example of a very human desire for noble ancestors as for example when Romans and Britons claimed descent from the Trojans.

Asturian churches show fundamental differences in ground plan and decoration and the invariable horseshoe arch of the Visigoths is not found until the late ninth century, when there was an influx of Mozarabs. On the outskirts of Oviedo, on the slopes of Mt Naranco, are two strange buildings. One is, or was, the palace of King Ramiro I (842–850); later it was converted into a church, Santa María de Naranco. Its architecture and decoration form one of our few links with the Dark Ages and the building deserves to be approached with the reverence owed to the unique. It is built of shaped stone, in two storeys, with barrel-vaulted ceilings; windows and porches tend to have three openings, separated by columns. The round arches that strengthen the vaults are buttressed on the outside (a constant feature of early Asturian buildings); alternate ones are continued inside as the twin spiral columns that separate the ornamental arcades along the walls. The primitive designs on the capitals are similar in all Asturian churches of the time. They make frequent use of cable decoration and may show Byzantine influence, but some see a resemblance between Asturian surface decoration and the art of the Vikings, who were at that time making repeated and unwelcome visits to the north of Spain.

The other building on Mt Naranco is San Miguel de Lillo, or Liño, probably the original palace chapel. (It has been suggested that the word Liño (Latin: *de ligno*) refers to a splinter of the True Cross (*lignum crucis*), of which relic St Michael was made guardian.) It is the sculptured decoration which will interest you most: herring-bone courses, spiral columns and perforated stone windows which many regard as derived from the Arab *Qamariyyah* but it is possible that both had a Roman or Byzantine origin (Similarly the cable ornamentation of Asturian buildings has Roman, Celtic and Scandinavian counterparts.) Best of all, on your right immediately inside the door, is an imitation in stone of an ivory consular diptych as used in the late Roman empire. This one shows the consul presiding over the games, his folded *mapa* in the right hand (bull fights are still started by the president laying a handkerchief over the front of his box), while an acrobat and a lion-tamer perform in another panel.

A third and earlier church, Santullana (St Julian), must have been gorgeous in its day for the whole interior was painted in fresco. The complete scheme of decoration can be seen in reproductions and is being brought back to life by skilful restoration. Parts remind one of the dwellings of Pompeii; others of the mosaics in San Apollinare Nuovo in Ravenna. It is significant that two Roman pilasters, used again in the con-struction of St Julian, harmonise with the themes painted in fresco. The origin of this early Asturian art may possibly be deduced by studying the barrel-vaults, buttresses and decoration; there are Roman and Byzantine precedents for all these and this ninth- and tenth-century art may therefore owe nothing to

Visigoths or Arabs. There are two other early Asturian churches which show how far the mountaineers had developed their art before the advent of the Romanesque style. One is easily seen, as it is next to the main road leading from Oviedo to León. Though only a hermitage, Santa Cristina de Lena shows many features that we saw in Santa María de Naranco – spiral columns, cable decoration and crude figures on the capitals and the external angled buttresses. Inside there is an altar screen with typical Visigothic patterns in relief; the inscription on the upper part is in Visigothic characters and is still not fully deciphered. Neither style nor inscription therefore suffice to date these marble slabs but they are obviously older than the hermitage and were brought there as an afterthought. The other pre-Romanesque church which repays travelling the extra distance from León is the later El Salvador of Valdedios. Completed in 893, it still shows traces of its original frescoes. The windows, both those that are divided by one or two mullions, and others that contain carved stone tracery, are especially worth noting. Here the horseshoe arch and other Visigothic characters re-appear, brought no doubt by Mozarab refugees; note especially the Asturian cable decoration combined with the Arab *alfiz*. At Santo Adriano de Tuñón (891) can be seen the earliest known Mozarabic frescoes portraying the stepped battlements which are a feature of Córdoba Mosque. A rare find. A last example of Mozarabic art is found in the Museum of Astorga; the lower part of this window frame has typically Visigothic, stumpy columns, the upper shows the lobulated arch that the Arabs brought from Iraq.

Attractive though these buildings may be, they are still primitive. You are therefore in no way prepared for the minor arts of the Asturian kingdom. The inscribed and gilded coffer for relics, given by Alfonso III to Astorga Cathedral about A.D. 900, is admirably preserved. True, it is rude compared with the Córdoba ivory carvings of the same period, but is still an artistic achievement, fit to be compared with similar western European contemporary productions. Even so it is inferior in workmanship to the Cross of the Angels in Oviedo Cathedral. To see this and many other things of beauty you must visit the Cámara Santa, a Holy of Holies that contains priceless relics; these were said to have been taken to Rome when the Persians under Chosroes II sacked Jerusalem (A.D. 614); from there they found their way to

A window at El Salvador
de Valdedios.

El Salvador de Valdedios.

A tripartite window at
El Salvador de Valdedios.

the Asturian kingdom, picking up on the way a cedarwood chest, silver-plated and with Arabic lettering. The relics themselves are so holy that pilgrims on the road to Santiago de Compostela usually made the extra and arduous journey to Oviedo.[2] These relics are responsible for the Cathedral of Oviedo, architecturally unremarkable, being known as *Sancta* in the Middle Ages. Here they saw, not only a piece of the True Cross and two thorns from Christ's crown, but St Peter's sandal and one of the thirty pieces of silver. The Saviour's shroud is shown to pilgrims on Good Friday and in September; another can be seen at rarer intervals in Turin Cathedral. The chest was officially opened before Alfonso VI and the Cid in 1075, to verify its contents; on a similar, but unauthorised occasion, the onlookers were blinded by the radiance of the articles.

As we are on the subject of miracles we may as well admire the Cross of the Angels, inscribed and presented by Alfonso II in 808. It is a beautiful example of gold filigree, encrusted with precious and semi-precious stones, including a Roman cameo. Its workmanship is so far in advance of that of the Visigothic goldsmiths that a Byzantine or Italian origin is suspected; this would agree with the view that the early Asturian kingdom owed little to an alleged Visigothic parentage. When young King Alfonso XIII visited Oviedo in 1901, he asked why the Cross of the Angels was so called.

"Because", replied the bishop, "it is said that the angels made it on this spot to reward King Alfonso the Chaste."

"And what ground is there for thinking so?" enquired the King.

"Señor," replied the prelate, "none whatever. The time for traditions is passing away."

The other contents of the Cámara Santa could occupy you for a whole day. The Cross of Victory, whose wooden core is said to have been carried by Pelayo at the Battle of Covadonga, is another magnificent specimen of the goldsmith's art, dated about a century after the Cross of the Angels. It was regarded as a symbol of the Reconquest and figures in the Asturian coat-of-arms. There is a precious tenth-century coffer of gold, silver and enamel and 82 peices of agate. The base shows the symbols of the evangelists between the arms of a Greek cross, reminiscent of contemporary illuminations. It is an example of Mozarabic influence and the date (910) coincides with the revolt of Ibn Hafsun, many of whose supporters were Mozarabs; this section was therefore subjected to persecution and many fled to Christian territories (Chapter 3). The coffer is supposed to have been given to Alfonso II by Charlemagne, as a token mark of their friendship; remember that the latter also exchanged fraternal greetings with the Omayyad emir of Córdoba and the Abbasid Caliph Haroun al-Rashid. Surely he can't have been on such good terms with all three. Perhaps the Bishop of Oviedo is right and it is time for traditions to pass away. Romanesque, Byzantine and Gothic diptyches – a remarkable crucifixion of the eleventh century, said to have been the property of Nicodemus (a miracle if ever there was one), and sundry other chests and jewels complete an unrivalled collection of mediaeval minor arts.

Although they belong to a later age and should therefore strictly be mentioned in the next chapter, superb examples of Romanesque sculpture are preserved in the approach to the Cámara Santa. The twelve apostles are arranged in pairs, six on each side of the barrel-vaulted passage that forms the antechamber. Carved of white stone, standing on decorated bases and surmounted by elaborate Romanesque capitals, they are attributed to the latter part of the twelfth century. Note the love which inspired the sculptor and the skill which enabled him to portray his kindliness and reverence. No two faces are the same. All are animated and show a realism that will not be met again for centuries – always excepting the wonderful figures on the Pórtico de la Gloria in Santiago de Compostela. It is for this reason that an attempt has been made to attribute them to the same sculptor, Master Matthew. Though the experts may detect fundamental differences between Asturian and Romanesque art, the spirit of devotion shines through all their simplicity; compare, for instance, some of the objects in the Cámara Santa with an ivory crucifixion of the tenth century, now shown in the Museum of San Marcos, León.

For those who value scenery and salmon fishing Asturias has much to offer. Make an expedition to Covadonga you excuse and go east from Oviedo. At Cangas de Onís you will see a thirteenth-century bridge over the brawling Sella, a sight to make any fisherman's heart quicken. Spain's Head of State, a keen sportsman, comes to these parts with a salmon rod for relaxation; you should follow his example. In these remote parts one also finds one of the purest derivations from the Latin, the grain store or *hórreo* (Lat: *Horreum*). They are small, rectangular stone buildings on stilts with ratguard discs. They have balconies where the grain (now chiefly maize) is dried before storage and they are cool and dry inside.

To visit Covadonga from León you may take the mountain road that passes over the Picos de Europa through a district where chamois, bears, ospreys, wild cats and vultures still abound. Going by Cisterna and Riaño you will never be out of sight of a river, first the sluggish Esla, broad and with lush, shady banks and grassy islands where horses and cattle graze; later the foaming, clear green torrents of the Upper Esla and its tributary the Deva whose source is your destination. Coming from the plains of León or Old Castile, you cross the vast *Campi Gothici* whose undulations, as you approach the hills, may be bare of all signs of man except where a ruined Moorish watch tower crowns an eminence. Then you are in the foothills and huge tracts of golden broom form a backdrop on either side. The clay hereabouts must have a peculiar property for the roof tiles gleam with what I can only call a pink opalescence and you feel that when night falls they will continue to emit a rosy glow.

At Covadonga you climb the valley through a forest which shades the rivulet and clings to the steep, rocky sides. As you approach the cave and the great rock face rises three hundred feet above you the big trees give way to holly and mountain oak, the rock edges soften with moss and ferns and wild olives grow out of the crevices. The road forms a dam across the very top of the valley and from it you can look up to the cave and the Chapel of the Virgin while the clear water pours out of the rock face and gathers in a shallow pool below you. When you turn and look down the valley, over the carpet of tree-tops to the grim, precipitous mountains, to the steep walls on either side and back again to the sheer rock behind you, it is plain that this is indeed the setting for a battle to the death with no refuge for the conquered and one sole possibility of survival — victory.

Climb the steps of the pink marble that crops out here and there in Asturias and exactly matches that of Verona, and you are in the cave. In recesses are the simple sarcophagi of Pelayo, his wife Gaudiosa, his daughter Ermesinda and his son-in-law Alfonso I. Covadonga is a national shrine and all day the coaches arrive and spill their laughing loads of girls and boys; They visit the great basilica on a spur of the mountain, take a quick look at the cave and then go down to the pool, where their gay chattering echoes from the rock in such volume that it must put to shame the war-cry of a hundred and eighty-seven thousand doomed Moslems. Many historians still regard the episode as a turning point in the history of Spain, if not of Europe. The cynic, however, may well feel that the limit of Islam's expansion in the West was reached at Poitiers and that, even if Covadonga had never been the scene of their first repulse, they would, in some other place have met insuperable obstacles to the total conquest of Spain. It is not often mentioned that the name Pelayo is more reminiscent of Celtiberian-Roman than of Visigothic origin; and still less often that the spokesman for the Moslems before the battle was none other than Archbishop Oppas, brother or nephew of Witiza, the last but one king of the Goths. It certainly needs a glut of heroism to cancel such disgrace.

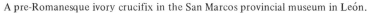

A pre-Romanesque ivory crucifix in the San Marcos provincial museum in León.

Burgos Cathedral.

CHAPTER TWELVE

The Pilgrims' Way: León and Burgos

The pilgrimage to Santiago de Compostela played a notable part in the story of the Reconquest, more perhaps than the problematical restoration of the Visigothic state. The early kings of León and Castile fought all their neighbours in turn, Navarrese, Galicians, Moslems and especially each other. It was religion that transformed them from a set of petty brigands to a united people with an urge to expand southward. Religion not only provided an ideal; it was instrumental in bringing civilising influences into the country, especially the monks of the rule of Cluny with all their skills. The Cluniacs came to look after the Road to Santiago and its pilgrims; they left their mark for all time in the Romanesque churches, so unmistakably French in style, that extend over northern Spain.

This is not the place to tell of the finding of the relics of St James the Greater (Santiago) nor of the the cult of pilgrimage which played such a part in mediaeval life. It suffices to say that the tomb was discovered early in the ninth century and that hordes of pilgrims were visiting Santiago de Compostela by 860. Every Christian country had its own routes by which pilgrims could reach far-off Galicia, almost as far from Rome as a Christian could get. Churches and chapels to St James still mark these roads: there is one at Winnenden near Stuttgart; Charlemagne's shrine at Aix-la-Chapelle shows the Emperor ready to follow the trail of stars that leads to Galicia, the *camino de Santiago* as the Milky Way is still called; the Rue St Jacques in Paris, the old south-west highway from the left bank, marks the pilgrims' path; and many a painting or carving of a mediaeval pilgrim identifies him by the scallop shell, the badge of St James.

Pilgrimage lent prestige and, like tourism today, brought money, even if the majority of pilgrims, like today's package tourists, had little to spend. At some time before the year 1000 the Spanish Moslems saw the advantages that a pilgrimage could bring; to compete with the pilgrimage to Mecca, an obligation for the devout Moslem, they publicised a foot-bone of Mohamed, derisively called the *zancarrón* by the Christians, kept in the Mosque of Córdoba. It was obviously an attempt at rivalling the Road to Santiago, for the latter brought strength to the northern kingdoms, not least in the guise of Templars and other fighting monks. Those of Islam, as we have seen in the case of the Almoravids, would have been better left uninvited, from the Spanish Moslems' point of view. It is impossible to do justice to the subject in the compass of a single chapter. But we can learn something of the early days of the northern kingdoms by visiting the capitals of León and Castile. You will remember that Castile began as a province, an off-shoot of León, which itself was the continuation of the Asturian kingdom; that it became a kingdom more powerful than its parent and that the two were not finally united until the days of St Ferdinand, who reconquered so much of al-Andalus in the thirteenth century. So let us see what remains of their ancient glories in the cities of León and Burgos.

LEÓN is the senior, but the younger brother Castile became more prominent, as branches from the old trunk are apt to do; note, for instance, the order in which they appear on Columbus' tomb (Chapter 7). It was a Roman foundation of about A.D. 70, the headquarters of the 7th legion (León = legion), situated on a secondary road. But with the neighbouring Asturica (Astorga) and Lucus (Lugo) it presented an offensive front to the wild Cantabrians, then, as in the time of the Moslem conquest, the most determined freedom fighters. All three cities preserve their defensive walls, in which Roman stones can be identified, least frequently in León. It was in 914 that Ordoño II moved his capital here from Oviedo, and thus re-established this court in the *Campi Gothici*, named after his presumed ancestors. Almanzor destroyed the city in 996, but some twenty years later Alfonso V rebuilt it. One of the still recognisable buildings was the Church of St John the Baptist, built over the remains of a monastery of St Pelagius (probably the boy-martyr of Córdoba, not the canonised Pope Pelagius II). Our interest begins when Ferdinand I of Castile conquered León and for the first time temporarily united the kingdoms (1035–65); note that his reign coincides with the final collapse of the caliphate and the emergence of the *taifa* kings. From now on there would be no more Almanzors; in the future the Moslems would pay tribute and the Christian kingdoms would largely subsist on this.

It was Ferdinand who sent Bishop Alvito to Seville to demand the body of St Justa (Chapter 4). For the consecrated home of her substitute's remains, the Church of St John was enlarged and named after St Isidore. The interment took place in 1063, in the presence of five other future saints, and miracles inevitably began; like the medical practitioner in a former part of the British Empire, his church could have hung out a sign: "Good for paralysis and deafness". These at least were the specialities with which Isidore was accredited by Lucas, Bishop of Tuy. His practice extended outside the city and there are stories of the body being taken far afield to arrest epidemics.

St Isidore's is one of the finest of the many Romanesque churches that stand by the Road to Santiago. It has all the exterior characters that you expect: it is squat and massive, its openings carry the typical semicircular arch, and its ornament is grouped round its portals. In the tympanum over the west entrance is a relief of typically sincere Romanesque style; it represents the thrilling moment during the sacrifice of Isaac when the angel (here represented by the Lord's hand) arrests Abraham in the act of killing his son and draws his attention to the ram in the thicket. To point out clearly the Christian significance of the Old Testament story, the sacrificial Lamb of God is shown above in a medallion, held up by two angels.

The interior of the church is equally massive, the column capitals richly carved, many of them exhibiting figures, human, animal and fabulous. Note the lofty scalloped arches into the transepts, a sign of Mozarabic or *mudéjar* participation found even in France. At the north-west, with a separate entrance, is the Chapel of Santa Catalina, or Pantheon of the Kings. It may have been, as Street surmised, the original church before the enlarge-ment needed to house its new relics. Certainly it gives a more

The tympanum of San Isidoro in León.

primitive impression, with stumpy columns and more coarsely carved capitals. But its chief glory, and indeed its fame, lies in the fresco paintings that cover walls, arches and celings. Though Marshal Soult's troops prised open the tombs in 1808 and helped themselves to the valuables, they for once forbore to deface the walls. Thus we are privileged to see what are undoubtedly the finest Romanesque paintings in Spain and among the best in the world. Here you can study the features typical of that epoch: observe the disproportion, so that some of the saints have the long, almost grotesque hands of an El Greco figure. Part of the vault is dedicated to religious subjects, the separation of the sheep from the goats, for instance; the bell wether has its bell attached to the muzzle, instead of round its neck. Bells are still attached in this way, at least to goats, in parts of the Leonese hill country. As usual, there is a massacre of the Innocents, the soldiers dressed in mediaeval chain mail holding up the victims by the hair, with the sword in the other hand. Just one, to be different, is holding his Innocent by the leg.

A set of twelve paintings represents the labours of the months. January is the most interesting, for you see a figure with two faces, opening a door with each hand — a representation of the Roman god Janus after whom the month is named. You are continually coming across evidence of classical knowledge in the

The vault of the High Constable's chapel in Burgos Cathedral.

Dark Ages: I regard it as originating in the same way as Romanesque art itself, in the desire to imitate the traces of Roman civilisation still existing at that time. The rest of the months deal with seasonal activities, pruning vines, planting, harvesting, threshing; in October the farmer is gathering acorns for the pigs, who are helping him with the task. November shows us the Martinmas slaughtering, for the eleventh was traditionally the day when surplus stock was killed and salted for the winter.

The museum-treasury is housed close to the Pantheon, in the adjacent bell tower. There is a marvellous collection of the minor arts: the Chest of the Ivories (1059); another of twelfth-century enamel; an ivory pyx a century older; linings of mediaeval Islamic textiles; chalices, one of them of agate; custodials; processional crosses − a paradise for the art lover. Observe, though, that the earlier exhibits portray exclusively French, Mozarabic or Islamic art; so far there is no indigenous school. But there is a wealth of illuminated manuscript books: a Job of the tenth century in visigothic script; a bible of the same age and style; another of the twelfth century, usually open at a miniature picturing David and Goliath, which should not be missed. Here is the real foundation of a native art and San Isidoro deserves high priority in a civilised holiday tour.

The Cathedral of León earns the adjective "beautiful" in *"Dives Toletana, pulchra Leontina, sancta Ovetensis, fortis Salamantina"*, and before ending our tour we shall have seen what ranked as Spain's premier cathedrals. This is the fourth to have been built over the baths of the 7th legion and dates from the thirteenth century. It is completely French in detail, in its plan and in its general design, as Street was the first to say. Here is a contrast to the Romanesque; everything is light and airy and one wonders how so little masonry can support so great a roof, itself constructed of special light materials with this object in mind. For the walls have been reduced almost to pillars, to make room for the vast expanse of stained glass which, in the sunlight of Spain, makes a jewel box of the interior. Almost every century is represented; one of the most interesting is the fifth upper window on the north side of the nave, a strangely secular product with castles, huntsmen, representations of the mediaeval scholars' *trivium* and *quadrivium*, falconers and women. There is much to be said for the belief that it once shone in the royal palace of St Ferdinand and was brought here when that building was demolished.

In the north transept is a chapel formerly named after the Virgin of the Die (*la Virgen del Dado*). The image itself is now to be found in an annexe to the north entrance. Her story is often repeated for its quaintness: a gambler, having invoked the help of the Virgin, was so annoyed at continuing to lose that he threw the dice at her image, upon which either she or the Child began to bleed. The miraculous aspect of the legend need not detain us; but it does confirm what so many travellers reported. First, that churches were used as a club or even as a social centre where the women could be ogled. And secondly, that saints are expected to do their job when invoked. From both Spain and Sicily there are reports of a saint's image being beaten or thrown into the river when prayers for rain had proved unavailing.

The Monastery of San Marcos, once a hospital for pilgrims, has been converted into a Plateresque palace housing a *de luxe* hotel. Its museum is well worth a visit (the illustration on p. 187 shows one of its treasures). For the English historian its most interesting exhibit is a letter from the High Admiral ordering the conscription of further men for the Armada and dated 4th July 1588; they were needed to replace the sick who had been put ashore at Corunna after the first attempt at sailing against England.

The Cathedral at BURGOS is, by contrast with that of León, simple, sober and solid. Again we could imagine ourselves in a French church; it is indeed probable that the original building had much in common with Rheims Cathedral. But additions and alterations have debased it and we now see what was once a noble, well-balanced construction choked by the addition of an arch-bishop's palace, and two sets of chapels of the fifteenth and sixteenth centuries. The pinnacles and spires were added in the fifteenth century; they make an impressive top to the west front, spoiled since 1790 by shoddy neo-classical portals. The lacy spires, so reminiscent of Freiburg im Breisgau, Strasbourg and, even more, Cologne, have their own story. Alonso de Cartagena, the cleric son of Pablo de Santa María, Jewish convert and Bishop of Burgos, attended the Council of Basle in 1431. He came back with the sculptor Juan de Colonia (Hans of Cologne). Having succeeded his father on the episcopal throne, Alonso commissioned the German in 1442 to complete the unfinished towers of Burgos Cathedral and add spires. German tourists rarely fail to marvel at their resemblance to the fretted spires of Cologne Cathedral. And well they may, for Hans of Cologne based his designs for Burgos on the plans for Cologne; these were lost for centuries and the spires of Cologne were built after their discovery in 1824. So here we have an example of a copy being four hundred years before the original.

The *Capilla del Condestable* (the Chapel of the High Constable of Castile) is worth seeing, if only for the riot of ornamentation that marked the transition from late, so-called Isabelline Gothic to Plateresque. Much of the work is by Diego de Siloé, son of the famous Gil, of Antwerp. And you will certainly have time to look at the great *Escalera dorada*, the double staircase by the same artist, that makes a stage setting of the north transept. Your best view of the interior is from the crossing, where you are next to the plain slab below the lantern that marks the tomb of the Cid and his wife Jimena.

Not far away, near the river, stands his gigantic statue, the noble beard flowing over chest and shoulders and we remember his vow never to trim it again after he was exiled. He thus became known

to minstrels as *barba vellida*, or "beautiful beard". At nearby
Vivar, where he was born, a statue by the roadside shows a much
younger Ruy Diaz with a puny beard. Not that we should expect
it to be a likeness, for the first "portrait" appeared late in the
sixteenth century, nearly five hundred years after his death. This
statue explains why he had to plait his beard and tuck it away
before battle; for the same reason Alexander made his
Macedonians shave, that the enemy might get no unfair advantage
by seizing the beard.

It is hard for us to realise the importance of a beard in man's
history; the Cid made a lifelong enemy of García Ordoñez, another
Castilian whom he found trying to extract tribute or "protection
money" from the Moslem vassal-king of Seville. This should have
been the Cid's job; Ordoñez was supposed to collect from the King
of Granada. After the ensuing battle, which the Cid won with
inferior numbers (did a hero's troops ever outnumber his
opponent's?), Ordoñez found himself a prisoner and high words
passed. In a moment of rage the Cid seized a handful of the other's
beard and tore it out by the roots. The old laws and privileges
regarded this as a serious injury and declared it a cause for
perpetual enmity. The Charter of Sepúlveda, in fact, went further
and fined the offender five *maravedíes*, or alternatively to have his
own beard plucked out; in the event of his being beardless, for
lawyers have to think of every contingency, an inch of skin was to
be cut out of the beard area. This is how the Cid incurred the
perpetual enmity of Ordónez and his noble supporters; through
them he lost the king's favour and I have no doubt that his rash
insult had a lot to do with his subsequent banishment.

The archaic *Poema de mio Cid* describes how he leaves his
beloved Burgos with his few faithful followers, heavy-hearted at
being exiled by his king. He turns to the cathedral and commends
his future to the Blessed Virgin: "Help me and protect me,
Glorious One, by night and day, and I shall send to your altar fine
gifts and rich and shall have a thousand masses said." The minstrel
is careful to remind us that the vow was fulfilled, just as we are
told (but on later authority) that he refunded to the Jews the
money borrowed on fraudulent security. All that the Jew Raquel
asked as interest, by the way, was "a piece of crimson leather,
Moorish and embroidered",which is proof, if any were needed, of
the superiority of Córdoban leather ware. This skill was un-

doubtedly derived from North Africa, where the tourist is to this day pestered to buy replicas of what the Jews of Burgos coveted in the year 1081.

Standing on the left bank of the Arlanzón today, you see none of the landmarks that met the Cid's eye when he turned Babieca's head towards the Cathedral. The impressive Arch of Santa María, the nearest point of entry to the Cathedral, carries a representation of the Cid among the heroes displayed. Burgos took part in the Comunero revolt of 1520 and its punishment was the erection, from its own funds, of the decorative gate tower that you see before you. There is, in fact, no tangible trace of the Cid today, except for an old parchment or two; but he lives in legend and history. Rodrigo, or Ruy Diaz de Vivar, better known as El Cid Campeador, was born in 1043 and died in 1099. In spite of painstaking historical research, which has been in progress for three hundred years, old fallacies die hard; though Menéndez Pidal succeeded in separating much of the chaff from the grain the Cid is still described, even in some Spanish reference books, as "semi-mythical". If they mean that a whole library of fancy has grown around his memory, they may be pardoned; but of his existence and the main outlines of his career we need have no doubts. Records relating to his life, written in his lifetime, are extant and the *Poema de mio Cid*, composed within forty years of his death, fits so well with Spanish and Arab authors that it may be regarded as documentary.

After a hundred years, however, the minstrels or *juglares* began to improve on history and produced a number of ballads, such as the *Mocedades*. These recounted episodes of a fictitious youth, partly concerning people who were dead before the Cid was born, and included the story of the duel and death of the imaginary Count Gómez Lozano and Rodrigo's subsequent marriage to the orphan daughter Jimena. As a good story it went the rounds of Europe while many truer, more important but less romantic episodes were forgotten. So eventually historians began to express doubts about the veracity of what they presented: *multa plura transcribo quam credo* wrote Mariana in the sixteenth century, and distrust grew so strongly that our protagonist and the mythical Bernardo del Carpio were bracketed as wholly imaginary characters. Quevedo and Cervantes opposed this view and in fact went to the opposite extreme, conferring reality on the mythical

Bernardo. In "Don Quixote" you may read, "That the Cid and no less Bernardo del Carpio existed there is no doubt, but I think that their exploits are exaggerated".[1]

The discovery of forgotten documents has been going on steadily since the eighteenth century and some of our most important information has come to light recently. A romantic interlude in Europe's taste for drama gave the Valencian Guillén de Castro y Bellvis the chance to write a sentimental piece about his own city's most famous character; Corneille eagerly adapted the theme to the French stage and gave Napoleon his favourite play. With the next romantic revival, in the nineteenth century, the legendary Cid returned to prominence. In Britain alone there were contributions by Southey, Lockhart and George Dennis, better known as a pioneer excavator in Etruria, whose "Chronicle of the Cid" was first published in "The Penny Magazine". A bit of a come-down, one would say, for the hero who was said to have received an embassy, laden with precious gifts, from the Shah of Persia. The Cid Campeador was so called from the Arabic title *Sidi* (Lord) and the Spanish for "champion", for we are speaking of the days when one or more warriors would ride out before the army and challenge a like number of opponents, the combat serving as a kind of *hors d'oeuvre* to the battle. The accusation, so often repeated, that the Cid was nothing but a gangster who did not hesitate to ally himself with the Moslems, is no longer impressive. The *taifa* kingdoms were clients of the various Christian kings. The Cid's alliance with Moslems was therefore an everyday event; remember also that it was less than a century since Almanzor's Christian allies had helped to destroy the sanctuary of Santiago de Compostela.

I have mentioned the treasure given to his bride Galla Placidia by the chieftain Ataulph, after the Visigoths had sacked Rome, traversed Italy and arrived in Narbonne. It represented the *morgincap* or reward for virginity. By the time of the Cid it had been adopted as a routine part of the marriage contract by the Spanish nobility. In the cathedral archives of Burgos you may see the original marriage contract between "Ruderigo Didaz" and "Scemena",[2] dated 19th July 1074 and witnessed by Aldefonsus gratia Dei Rex (Alfonso King by the Grace of God), Hurracka (Urraca) and many others. At the head of the twentieth page you find *"ob decorem pulcritudinis et federe matrimoni virginalis connubii*". This refers to the reward for beauty and/or virginity and is hence a descendant of the *morgincap*; in this instance Rodrigo could hardly do less than mention both, for he was marrying into the royal house. His descendants, through a daughter, have been traced and include in the sixth generation two saints Ferdinand III of León and Castile, and Louis IX of France.

These should not be confused with the descendants of the daughter's first husband, a coward and a scoundrel who, with his brother, came courting the Cid's daughters. They say that one day, while the Cid was enjoying his siesta, a lion broke out of its cage; even while the rest gathered round to protect their chief the suitors made off, one under a bed and the other behind a wine-press, whence "he brought out his cloak and kirtle all soiled", as the *Poema* puts it. The Cid woke up and without fuss took the lion by its mane and conducted it back to its cage. The story puts me in mind of the strange resemblances between the heroes of Spain and Scotland: the Cid and Robert Bruce. Of the latter it is said that he too had a tame lion, and there are records that its cage cost £1 13s 0d and its food £6 13s 4d a year. Both heroes are unjustly accused of changing sides when it suited them. Both were exiled and had to leave their wives behind, the one at San Pedro de Cardenas, the other in Kildrummie Castle. Bruce was at one time praised and rewarded by Edward I of England, at another accused of being faithless and inconstant. The same changes marked the relationship of Ruy Diaz and Alfonso VI. Bruce was certainly excommunicated for the murder of the Red Comyn in the church of the Greyfriars at Dumfries; Ruy Diaz was excommunicated, but only in narratives that circulated centuries after his death. Both were described as brave and strong, masters of the art of war, generous and courteous: witness the Cid's behaviour to the boastful Count of Barcelona, who changed his tune when he found himself a prisoner after a lost battle. Bruce's generosity to the gallant Sir Marmaduke de Twenge and other English knights, after the battle of Bannockburn, was equally characteristic. Again, during his campaign in Ireland, about the year 1318, Robert Bruce was conducting a hasty retreat from the allied English and Irish, when he heard a woman's shrieks. Sir Walter Scott recounts how the King asked the reason and was told that a washerwoman, having just given birth to an infant, was to be left behind, too weak to travel. The mother was shrieking at the thought of falling into the hands of the Irish and Bruce refused to continue the retreat, risking a battle against overwhelming odds "rather than leave these poor creatures behind me."[3]

Now let us go back two hundred years, to the Spain of autumn 1081. The Cid was in the early days of his exile, surrounded by the hostile forces of Zaragoza, Aragón and Castile; against the last he would not, in any case, fight ("*Con Alfonso mio señor non querria lidiar*", says the *Poema*) and rapid movement seemed essential. As they were striking camp in the morning he overheard someone remark that the cook's wife had given birth to an infant during the night: "How many days", he asked, "do the ladies of Castile rest in bed after their confinement?" When they told him he continued, "Then for so many days more shall our tents remain here."

Burgos has an excellent museum and in a cellar is the tomb of Juan de Padilla — not the one who was executed after the revolt of the communes in 1520, but the squire whom Queen Isabel used to call affectionately "*mi loco*", and who was killed during the siege of Granada. It is the work of the renowned Gil de Siloé, father of Diego; it is late, "degenerate" Gothic and marked by the lavish use of alabaster. If you like it you can see other examples of Siloé's work near Burgos: at Miraflores, the Carthusian monastery, are the tombs of Isabel's parents; you have already seen some of the younger Siloé's work in the Cathedral. Sitwell has put forward a plausible conjecture that Gil was Jewish and, if he is right, then he is also correct in remarking that father and son were "the only considerable artists of Jewish origin to appear in Europe before the twentieth century."[4]

But the climax of your visit, to ensure which any of the foregoing attractions may be sacrificed, is the Convent of Las Huelgas; its full name, Santa María la Real de las Huelgas, reminds us it was the original gift of a royal holiday resort to house a hundred nuns of aristocratic birth. Wealth and privilege made it something of an exclusive club, in fact Cardinal Aldobrandini, in the late sixteenth century, remarked that if the Pope ever married he could not find a more suitable wife than the abbess of Las Huelgas. The latter, herself sometimes of royal blood, ruled over fifty-one towns and thirteen subsidiary convents. When Baron Rosmithal, brother-in-law of the King of Bohemia, visited Las Huelgas in 1465, "most beautiful nuns, all of high lineage ...

entertained him with games and other diversions, such as dances, songs and similar things, and showed him into beautiful gardens full of trees and exquisite plants."[5]

The convent was founded in 1180 by Alfonso VIII, later the victor of Las Navas de Tolosa, and his wife Eleanor of Lancaster and England, daughter of our Henry II and Eleanor of Aquitaine. Street points out that architectural details are reminiscent of Poitou and Anjou, which belonged to the English crown; they could also derive from Aquitaine, so that Eleanor could have got her builders anywhere south of Brittany. The observation is not a trivial one, for the style was widely copied in Spain, even as far away as Barcelona. The buildings were originally Romanesque, then transitional and Gothic features appeared, and anywhere one is likely to be confronted with *mudéjar* details, a pointed horseshoe arch, an *artesonado* or stucco ceiling with an Arabic inscription. Even the merlons of the battlements have the pyramidal Almohad cap.

The Arco de Santa María in Burgos.

Much as I should like to describe this Cistercian convent in more detail, the contents must have priority for they are almost a summary of Castile's mediaeval history. The royal tombs, beginning with those of the founders in the nave of the church, should have precedence. Some of them were overlooked by the French looters and have yielded an amazing variety of textiles, mostly with oriental designs, and of clothing accessories. Here too is the skull of Henry I, only son of the founders, who died in his teens from injuries caused by a falling roof-tile. One can see that an effort was made to save his life by trephining, an operation as old as mankind. And here is the tent-flap of the Almohad caliph defeated at Las Navas. The rest of the tent was sent to Rome as a trophy, for it was Pope Innocent III who had urged the squabbling Christian states to combine for once. So it happened that all played their part: the Templars fought devotedly and their losses were the heaviest; the Navarrese broke the living barrier of the negro bodyguard and carried off the chain which surrounded the caliphal tent, whence it became incorporated into the royal arms and so into those of Spain three centuries later.

The last object that I have selected from such a wealth of interest is the articulated thirteenth-century statue of St James in the little *mudéjar* chapel of Santiago. He carries a sword and it is believed that the effigy was used to give the accolade to those whose royal blood precluded their being dubbed by anyone of baser fibre. This, of course, required the help of an operator hidden under the platform. You will remember that Edward I was knighted at Las Huelgas, but this was at the hands of the King of Castile himself. Here, too, kings were crowned, and in 1367 the Black Prince lodged, while preparing a treaty with Pedro the Cruel after Navarrete (Chapter 6). How closely the royal houses were connected! John of Gaunt, brother of the Black Prince, later claimed the throne of Castile through his marriage with Pedro's daughter. And long, long before, soon after Alfonso VIII founded the convent of Las Huelgas, his first cousin Berenguela was to marry his English brother-in-law Richard Coeur-de-Lion.

CHAPTER THIRTEEN

The Renaissance in Spain: Salamanca

The most beautiful square in Spain — the finest Renaissance buildings — the most complete anthology of artistic styles. Claims ancient and modern; the only wonder is that they are true. Take the Plaza. Imagine four sides of creamy stone in restrained Baroque, all on deep, cool arcades, all matching and all beautiful. At one end the Town Hall rises above the third storey and houses the clock, the servant of man — at least in Spain. When man becomes the slave of time they believe here, clocks will make men. I don't know the dimensions but the square must be at least as large as the great Plaza Mayor of Madrid. Both are relics of the eighteenth century and both rose over traces of earlier plazas. Man being by nature conservative, the plaza often perpetuates the site of the Roman forum.

On the east side the royal pavilion rises above the *arco del toro*, through which bulls were loosed into the plaza to make sport for, and with, the cavaliers. In 1467 Rosmithal, whom we met at Las Huelgas, saw the bull-fight that marked the July feast of Santiago. Then, of course, the plaza was of a different style and the bull-fight of the old kind in which mounted men rode against the bulls, relying on their own accuracy with the spear and the agility of their mounts. On that occasion one bull alone killed two men and wounded eight, and one horse was wounded. A more sporting effort than the modern fighting on foot, which developed about the time this plaza was built and became a loathsome slaughter-house for worn-out horses until 1928.

This is not a guide book and I cannot show you more than a
sample of what Salamanca holds, but I would nevertheless advise
taking a route that leaves the Plaza Mayor at the south-west
corner. In a moment you come on the Church of San Martín,
which is itself a miniature history book. The north portal, which
faces you, has a Romanesque relief of the old theme of St Martin
cutting his cloak to share it with a beggar. Had he been a Spaniard
instead of a Frenchman, they say, he would have given away the
whole cloak. Now go round to the south portal and see the same
subject treated by a Renaissance sculptor; the comparison gives
the amateur all the practical help he needs in appreciating the vast
difference between the twelfth and sixteenth centuries. Inside
there is yet another feature of interest, a thirteenth-century arch,
part of the older west façade, now being exhumed from its grave
inside later additions under the *coro*, or raised choir. One of St
Martin's old names was *San Martín de la Plaza*, another reminder
that the great square stood where it does at the time of the
Reconquest in the eleventh century. It was soon after Alfonso VI's
conquest of Toledo that his son-in-law, Raymond of Burgundy,
undertook the repopulation of the deserted town. Seven groups of
colonists were settled, each in its own quarter; among them were
Franks and Portuguese, Castilians and Mozarabs, and each had its
own parish church. Bishop Jerome of Poitiers was given responsibility for them all. He was a fighting bishop and had accompanied
the Cid on several campaigns, finally helping him to capture
Valencia. He and the Cid's widow Jimena arranged that the Cid's
body was brought back to Castile when Valencia had to be
surrendered to the Almoravids. Thus you may find seven churches
of Romanesque construction in Salamanca; your enjoyment will
be heightened by remembering that the *mudéjar* Church of
Santiago near the bridge marks the parish of the Mozarabs, just as
the ruined Church of St Thomas of "Cantorbery" reminds us that
the English colony lived in that area and built the church only
three years after Beckett's canonisation, or five after his murder.
The finest of all is the Old Cathedral, only a short walk from St
Martin's.

But you are here, at least partly, in search of Renaissance and
especially Plateresque monuments, and you will not be disappointed, for there are many to be seen. And on the
way down the Calle de la Rua Mayor you must watch for an

open space on the right and turn in to see the celebrated *Casa de las Conchas*, the House of the Shells. It is a harmonious example of the era when the conservative Spaniard could hardly bear to abandon the Gothic style he had used to such effect for so long, in order to adopt the Renaissance. This usually took the form of "Plateresque", so called because the details remind one of the work of the *platero* or silversmith. The solution was naturally to combine the styles, adding a touch of *mudéjar* and finishing with a palace which is sheer delight, both inside and out. The shells are an original form of decoration in an age when fancy was free and external ornament in pyramidal or other shape was commonplace. Note the wrought-iron grilles, dignified yet elegant, that cover the lower windows and enhance the front view.

The house was built by a Maldonado, who came by his name in a curious fashion. The family of Arias de Talavera was represented from 1474 to 1512 by one Rodrigo, counsellor to Queen Isabel and ambassador at the court of King Louis XI in Paris. He became so popular that the king told him to name a wish, on which Rodrigo boldly asked for the privilege of including five fleurs-de-lis in his escutcheon. The request was granted reluctantly and you can see the result in the illustration; the king was heard to remark that it was unwisely given – *mal donné*, whence the new family name of Maldonado.[1] It was not long before the founder's grandson Francisco achieved fame of another kind by being executed when the revolt of the Communes was suppressed.

The name of the house was easy to choose. I have not seen the shells explained elsewhere, except in such vague terms as "the badge of the builder." They are there because Rodrigo was a knight of Santiago and therefore entitled to a scallop shell or two, while his wife was duchess of Benavente, who mounted ten scallop shells in *her* escutcheon. An old legend is still believed in Salamanca, that there is a treasure in gold pieces under one of the stone shells. It arose in this way: on the opposite corner is the Seminario, now the Universidad Pontificia, and while it was being built in 1617 the Jesuits wanted to pull down the Casa de las Conchas. The Maldonados would not agree and the Jesuits increased their offer until it stood at one ounce of gold for each scallop shell pulled down. Even this was refused but it gave rise to the belief that Jesuit gold was stored under a *concha*.

The interior presents the best features of Spanish Renaissance architecture. The courtyard has the usual two storeys, but the lower arcade is made up of joined segments of circles, a distinctly oriental touch. The whole is a monument to the wealth and taste of the Castilian aristocrat, but don't look too closely round the corner, where mean shops have recently been built into the imposing structure.

The Old Cathedral, of the early twelfth century, shares with the Plaza Mayor the honour of attracting most sightseers. From outside, even though a good view is difficult to get past the bulk of the New Cathedral (for the two are joined like Siamese twins), the strange lantern is the most striking feature. It is called the Cock Tower (*Torre del Gallo*) because it used to have a weathercock, the fowl being the national emblem of the French, to whom this parish had been apportioned. Since 1900, when the weathercock fell down, the Salamantines call it the "Chicken Tower". The strange shape of the lantern that illuminates the crossing as well as the four corner towers are also seen in Zamora, Toro and elsewhere, especially in the south-west of France. The basic style and even the scale covering of stone slabs arranged like scalloped shingles, is common to all the examples; it is said to have been brought from the Near East by the crusaders. Although one apse is partly buried in the New Cathedral, the two that remain are attractive in their simplicity and their slit-like, round-arched windows protected by twelfth-century forged iron grilles. Here you can compare a Romanesque exterior with the adjacent south transept façade of the New Cathedral, "spotted all over with niches, crockets and pedestals in the most childish way; whilst every spandrel has a head looking out of a circle, reminding one forcibly of the old application of a horse collar . . ."[2] Street can be very scathing; you may feel differently about the contrast, but you will agree that the massive Romanesque structure (whence the old *fortis Salamantina*) contrasts with the lighter and loftier Gothic.

If you are in the right mood you will profit by wandering at will through the Old Cathedral and forgetting the Renaissance for a while. Here are examples of thirteenth-century fresco, the colours skilfully restored, in the Chapel of St Martin, also called the Oil Chapel; being without direct daylight it was found suitable for the storage of olive oil, an important item since it was the only source of illumination. Look at some of the capitals and admire their

The Plaza Major at Salamanca.

delicate workmanship; the local stone has the property of being soft and easily worked when freshly quarried, hardening later and lasting indefinitely. There are examples of a mythical creature, a bird with a woman's head, found in many Romanesque churches in Western Europe. In Spain they are called "Sphinxes"; elsewhere "Sirens"; the former is nearer to the truth, but only by chance: they are the original Ba of Ancient Egypt, the soul of the departed that lives with the gods but comes down at intervals to comfort the mummy. They probably came to Europe through the Sassanid art of Persia and the Crusades. It is strange how often they are seen on capitals near a tomb, as though their original function had never been quite forgotten.

Further up the cathedral there are more painted tombs, but the eye is held by the enormous, elaborate and beautiful retable, painted near the middle of the fifteenth century. The artist, usually called Nicola Florentino, was probably the Italian Dello Delli (Daniello Nicolo Delli). There are fifty-three compartments filled with episodes from the life of Christ, all of equal merit. Note the competent handling of perspective and see especially the "Visitation", in which each expectant mother has a tiny manikin painted in where you might expect. There is plenty of history, too, in the chapels round the beautiful cloister. Try to disregard the damage caused by the earthquake of 1755, which wrecked Lisbon, and well-meaning but bungling restorations and look at such Romanesque work as has survived in its original form, among the legacies of the Renaissance. The first chapel on the left is named after "Doctor Talavera", actually our friend the Maldonado who built the House of the Shells. Our breath will be taken away first by the alabaster effigies and wrought-iron grille of the tomb in the centre; then we are shown a flag, the tattered remains of one which the Comuneros of 1520 carried in their fatal attempt to secure home rule in a hurry; you will remember that a Maldonado was among the few leaders who suffered the death penalty. Finally you should study the ceiling, with its vault criss-crossed by pairs of parallel ribs that leave an octagonal space free in the centre. The earliest Spanish example is the one we saw before the *mihrab* in Córdoba; it probably represents the origin of rib vaulting in European church architecture but has survived in few buildings in this form; one is the little church in Torres del Río (Navarre). In this chapel, six services of the Mozarabic rite are held each year, just as Toledo has a daily one.

The Chapel of Santa Bárbara is notable for the fact that University examinations were formerly conducted in it, the candidate having spent the previous night in prayer and study over the central tomb. The door by which the unsuccessful were ushered out is appropriately called "*La puerta del burro*", a variant of *pons asinorum* no doubt. The Diocesan Museum is here too and for those who feel pictures essential to the osmosis of culture there are many examples of Fernando Gallego, "the Spanish Van Eyck". He and his brother Francisco were among the first to adopt the Flemish style of painting but they gave it a dramatic quality which is quite Spanish. This is the city to see their work, for they were born here. If you want light relief look for the picture of a custom that lasted until recently in Salamanca. For ten days women used to exchange their newborn baby for an older one, Heaven knows on what pseudo-scientific grounds; the only one that occurs to me is that a more vigorous infant might increase the flow of milk. In any case, in an old retable from nearby Terravillas, painter unknown, you can see the older child's jealousy of the "cuckoo".

If you were impressed by the *reja* in the Talavera Chapel, the one surrounding the tomb of the Anaya will give you a fresh thrill.

The organ in the corner is of the fifteenth century and its casing is decorated in *mudéjar* style with geometric patterns and ornamental bosses. There is another organ, too, said to have belonged to the blind musician Salinas, friend of Luis de León, but it is to be seen only for its associations, not for its intrinsic beauty.

The Gothic age died hard in Spain and the New Cathedral is one of the latest to be built in this style, at a time when the rest of Europe was plunged in the Renaissance. Outside, it is undoubtedly spoiled by second thoughts, for Renaissance and Baroque sculpture has been added to Street's "childish niches, crockets and pinnacles." But the noble proportions of the interior must heighten your admiration, already aroused by the pure colour of the stone. Don't forget to ask for the Crucifix of the Cid, for, in a chapel exhibiting the worst excesses of Churrigueresque Baroque decoration in gilt, hangs the simple, dark and strangely beautiful figure of a Romanesque Christ on the Cross. It is said to have been carried into battle with the Cid and the story is a likely one, for we have seen how the Old Cathedral was begun under the supervision of the Cid's friend, comrade in arms and confessor, Bishop Herome of Poitiers. What more natural than that he would bring with him to Salamanca the crucifix he had so often followed in battle?

But Salamanca's main glory has always been the University, whose statutes were approved by the Spanish Antipope Benedict XIII. Founded in the thirteenth century, during which it also achieved wide fame, the present buildings date from the time of the Catholic Sovereigns. Here is the Spanish Renaissance in all its phases. The main façade (p. 212) is by itself a sufficient dose of the Plateresque in which the *alfiz* has developed into a riot of decoration, the *horror vacui* that likewise came from the Orient. The show pieces inside that I like best are the panelled ceiling round the courtyard, with typical *mudéjar* geometric patterns and vivid colours, and the monumental staircase with its flowers and bees which is probably simply exuberance and devoid of symbolism. But the bull-fight at the turn of the stair represents the old method, with mounted cavalier and bull prodded on by a manservant; the same mounted herdsmen are credited with victories over Napoleon's troops in the Peninsular War.

Up in the library, a bibliophile's dream, is a chest with five locks in which the University's funds were kept at one time. Each lock

The chair of Fray Luis de León
at Salamanca University.

had a different key and each key was in the keeping of a different
official. In spite of these precautions, however, the pedants were
outwitted and the chest rifled; hence its name of *Arca boba* or
booby chest. Perhaps this library was imagined as the scene of the
apocryphal confrontation of Columbus and the professors who
were to give an opinion on his project. As children we were told
that they denied the earth was round, for if this were so it would
have no stability. Columbus confounded them by tapping the
famous egg (did he come with it in his pocket?) until the shell
flattened at the pole and thus made it stand upright. The belief
that the earth was round was nothing new; what the Salamanca
experts were questioning was Toscanelli's estimate of the earth's
circumference. They were right too, for Toscanelli – and
Columbus – thought that the distance to Japan, going westwards,
was about a third of its actual figure. Had America not been
providentially placed, the explorers of those days could never have
made a landfall.

But perhaps the most notable visit to be made in Salamanca is
to the classroom in which Luis de León lectured. Over the door is
a Hebrew text whose time-honoured translation reads, "Happy are
thy men, happy are these thy servants, which stand continually
before thee and hear thy wisdom." The dais and benches are
obviously those of the sixteenth century and we can almost hear
his opening words after five years in the dungeons of the
Inquisition, *"Dicebamus hesterna die ..."* – "we were saying

yesterday." Almost. In actual fact, his chair had been filled by another during his absence and he was not reappointed, though a substitute chair was found for him in another faculty. But there is an aura in the lecture hall. Here, we can say, the great have trodden, Ignatius de Loyola, Calderón de la Barca, Peter Martyr — but perhaps "trodden" is the wrong word, for the crowd that came to hear the last-named's introductory lecture on a satire of Juvenal was so thick that he had to be passed over their shoulders to the dais. Spain thronged to hear this immigrant Italian's opinions and profited by his learning, though he never reached the clarity of thought and purity of language achieved by Luis de León.

We can learn a lot about Spain, mostly to the country's advantage, from briefly considering the life of León. He was a disciple of Garcilaso de la Vega, which makes him a late arrival in the galaxy of the Spanish literary Renaissance. His was the most harmonious, balanced and perfect writing of the Golden Century, a wedding of intellect and emotion. "No one has flown so high . . .", wrote that stern but just critic Menéndez y Pelayo. León was an Augustinian monk and consequently embroiled in the rivalry between his order and the Dominicans. As the latter were the executives of the Spanish Inquisition, it is not surprising that the brilliant León was denounced by unsuccessful rivals and imprisoned by the Holy Office. The charges were, first, that he had secretly translated the Song of Solomon and second, that he had disparaged the authority of the Vulgate. The latter accusation was based on the fact that, like Milton, León knew Hebrew and was in a position to detect errors in Jerome's work; the former was made under the mistaken impression that he enjoyed pornography. Well, according to modern critics, he probably did, without knowing it. The Song of Songs is believed by many to be a rather frank oriental love poem that got into the Old Testament by mistake; but in León's day it was regarded as allegorical and St John of the Cross, to give only one example, based much of his mystical poetry on it.

To make the accusation stick his opponents were not above alleging that he had a Jewish great-grandmother. The Inquisition went into the case thoroughly, taking nearly five years to do so; meanwhile León produced his prose masterpiece "The Names of Christ". In criticising the delay we are apt to forget the

The façade of
Salamanca University.

importance attached to philosophy and belief in the days before
newspapers and books disseminated opinions. Not for them such
articles as "What the well-read man is thinking". His case was no
easy one to judge. In both prose and poetry he is regarded as one
of the finest Spanish writers of all time. To him Horace was the
perfect lyrical poet and it was love of the classical masters that
resulted in his flawless translations into everyday Castilian. Like
Horace he sighed for the quiet country life, away from care, but
where Horace (*Epodes* II,1) expresses this desire and later claims
immortality for his work (*Odes*, III, xxx, 1), León contents
himself with the desire alone. On the wall of a house near Alba de
Tormes is engraved the poem that he wrote on his release from
prison: —

> Here envying and lies
> Held me shut fast.
> Happy his simple state
> Who, wise at last,
> To this ill-dealing world himself denies,
> And with poor board and bed

The Palace of Los Duques del Infantado at Guadalajara, begun in 1461.

In the sweet countryside
By only God is tried,
And lives his life alone,
None envying him, and he not anyone.

(Brenda Sackett's translation)

The resemblance to Horace does not end there. León took the *lira* metre of Bernardo Tasso for his few poems, so that where Horace boasted that he was the first to fit the lyrics of Greece to the Italian measure, León forbore to point out that he was the first to fit Italian lyrics to the rhythm of Castilian. Our verdict must be that he dreamed of a heaven where music and Platonic order combined with Christian faith; he erred in believing that this heaven could be found on earth: certainly it was far from the rough-and-tumble of theological dispute in Salamanca University and further still from the interrogation chambers of the Inquisition.

By now you will be asking what we can learn to Spain's advantage from a brilliant monk who was unjustly imprisoned for five years. First, I would say, the fact that he was released by the

Inquisition and never subjected to torture. This, the cynic might reply, was simply because he had no money. On the other hand we must remember that torture was a normal part of sixteenth-century judicial procedure; but, when the artist Alonso Cano was examined by the Inquisition, his right hand was scrupulously spared and he too was acquitted. The fact is that León, even though unjustly accused and imprisoned, did eventually obtain justice. Second, the University did its best to make restitution and his Order, the Augustinians, supported and promoted him after his release. There are few modern countries where imprisonment, even if unjust, does not smear the victim and prejudice his future. Third, the poet Quevedo published León's works to show how lyrics should be written. This was in the 1620s, when the political climate was even less liberal and the Inquisition as active as ever. And last, his works have been read and loved in Spain to the present day; there he has always been regarded as typifying that combination of elegant style and mysticism that marked the Spanish Renaissance.

These are but the better known attractions of Salamanca. The bridge over the Tormes is one of Spain's, and the world's best examples of Roman construction. The Torre del Clavero, with its bartisan turrets, marks the end of the Middle Ages, and is a late example of a type of defence that proved useless against cannon. Wellington is said to have surveyed the battlefield of Salamanca from its summit; I don't believe it. Before the battle he ignored the Arapiles, where the engagement was fought; its site was determined by a stupid manoeuvre on Marmont's part; and during the battle he was with the leading regiment of the Light Division. If you are interested in Renaissance-Plateresque architecture and decoration, there is a wealth of buildings you can study as you walk about the town. The present Provincial Museum was the house of Doctor Abarca Maldonado, physician to Isabel the Catholic; it has also been called the House of Brother Luis de León, but the title is accurate only in so far as it refers to his being confessor to the owner's wife. Here, well into the sixteenth century, you can detect the reluctance with which Gothic was abandoned in favour of Renaissance. This applies to the Irish College, or College of the Archbishop, of 1534—49. A magnificent Renaissance patio and a Gothic chapel complement each other, the latter showing by its purely ornamental vault ribbing that its day was done. The Irish fathers were those who came to study at the University of Salamanca; the building was set aside for them in 1578, which is when Philip II began to get really annoyed with the Protestant England of Queen Elizabeth I. No doubt it produced a number of learned clerics; it is chiefly remembered for the introduction of football into Spain.

If I omit of many of the houses whose imposing fronts make your wanderings through Salamanca so pleasant, it is only because they are so numerous. But it would be worth your while to take a short walk north from the Plaza Mayor to the Plaza de los Bandos. The "bands" or factions were the curse of Salamanca, analogous to the Montagues and Capulets of Verona. Here they were represented by the parishes of Saints Thomas and Benedict. In No. 7 of the Plaza, the house with three crests carved in stone and the arched entrance with its huge mediaeval voussoirs, lived María de Monroy, a widow, with her two sons, direct descendants of St Ferdinand, King of León and Castile. The sons were murdered by the Benedictine faction and the two assassins fled to Portugal. María buried her sons, put on her dead husbands armour and rode to Portugal with an escort of her retainers. In Viseu she caught up with her quarry, fought them, killed them and rode back, to throw their heads on her sons' graves. It is still called the House of Dona María la Brava. And in front of its creamy stone, its *alfiz* and its iron balcony – all so typically Spanish – we can fittingly take leave of "this intrepid people, whose women fought like men. . . ."

Zamora Cathedral.

Further Reading

(*indicates Spanish or French texts)

Atkinson, W. C. *A History of Spain and Portugal*, Penguin, London 1960

Beckwith, J., *Caskets from Córdoba*, H.M.S.O., London 1960

*Berenguer, Magin, *Arte en Asturias*, Grandio, Oviedo 1969

Bernaldo de Quirós, F. T., *The Spanish Jews*, Rivadeneyra, Madrid 1961

Berruete, M. D., *León*, Aries, Barcelona 1962

Borrow, G., *The Bible in Spain,* Dent (Everyman's), London 1906

Brenan, G., *The Face of Spain*, Turnstile Press, London 1950

Brenan, G., *The Literature of the Spanish People*, Penguin, London 1952 (2nd edition)

*Cabezas, J. A., *Asturias*, Aries, Barcelona 1966

*Cervantes Saavedra, M. de, *El ingenioso hidalgo Don Quixote de la Mancha*, Sopena, Barcelona 1961 (First published 1604. English translation by J. M. Cohen, Penguin Classics, London 1950)

*Cervantes Saavedra, M. de, *La Numancia*, Aguilar, Madrid 1964

Condé, J. A., *History of the Dominion of the Arabs in Spain*, 3 vols, translated by Mrs J. Foster, Bohn, London 1854

Durant, W., *The Story of Civilization:* (3)`Caesar and Christ* (4) *The Age of Faith* (5) *The Renaissance* (6) *The Reformation*, Simon & Shuster, New York 1944–57

Espinas, J. M., *Tarragona*, Noguer, Barcelona 1964

Flores, A., *An Anthology of Spanish Poetry*, Doubleday, New York 1961

Ford, R., *Gatherings from Spain*, Dent (Everyman's), London 1970

Ford, R., *Handbook for Travellers in Spain*, 3 vols, reprinted Centaur, London 1966

Ford, R., *Murray's Handbook for Travellers in Spain*, John Murray, London 1882 (6th edition)

Froissart, J., *The Chronicles of England, France, Spain, etc.*, Routledge, London 1891

*Gabarda, E., *Historia de los Amantes de Teruel*, Perruca, Teruel 1963 (10th edition)

García Mercadel, J., *Viajes de extranjeros por España y Portugal*, 3 vols, Aguilar, Madrid 1952

Gaya Nuño, J. A., *Burgos*, Aries, Barcelona n.d.

Gibbon, E., *Decline and Fall of the Roman Empire*, Dent (Everyman's), London 1910

*Gudiol Ricart, J., *Tarragona y su Provincia*, Aries, Barcelona n.d.

Gudiol Ricart, J., *The Arts of Spain*, Thames & Hudson, London 1964

Hare, A. J. C., *Wanderings in Spain*, Smith, Elder & Co., London 1885 (5th edition)

Harvey, J., *The Cathedrals of Spain*, Batsford, London 1957

Hinde, T., *Spain*, Newnes, London 1963

Irving, W., *A Chronicle of the Conquest of Granada*, London 1910

*La Rada y Delgado, J. de Dios de, *Mujeres célebres de España y Portugal*, 2 vols, Espasa-Calpe, Buenos Aires 1954 (3rd edition)

*Lévi-Provençel, E., *La civilización ciárabe en España*, Espasa-Calpe, Buenos Aires 1953 (See also in Menéndez Pidal's *Historia de España. vols 4 & 5)*

Livermore, H., *A History of Spain*, Allen & Unwin, London 1958

*Lojendio, L. M. de, *Gonzalo de Córdoba (El Gran Capitán)*, Espasa-Calpe, Madrid 1942

Macaulay, R., *Fabled Shore*, Hamish Hamilton, London 1949

Macdonell, A. G., *Napoleon and his Marshals*, Macmillan, London 1934

*Mâle, E., *L'Art Religieux du XIIe Siècle en France*, Armand Colin, Paris 1922

*Mâle, E., *L'Art Religieux du XIIIe Siècle en France*, Armand Colin, Paris 1922

*Manzano, R., *Los Grandes Capitanes Españoles*, Gasso, Barcelona 1960

*Marañón, G., *Elogio y nostalgia de Toledo*, Espasa-Calpe, Madrid 1966 (4th edn)

*Marañón, G., *Ensaya biológico sobre Enrique IV de Castilla y su tiempo*, Espasa-Calpe, Madrid 1969 (11th edn)

*Marañón, G., *Las Ideas biológicas del P. Feijóo*, Madrid 1962 (4th edn)

*Marañón, G., *Tiempo viejo y tiempo nuevo*, Espasa-Calpe, Madrid 1965 (9th edn. N.B. it is important to get this or later editions which contain the story of Zobeida's Girdle in "La historia de las piedras".)

*Mariana, J. de, *Historia de España*, Ebro, Zaragoza 1955 (4th edn)

*Menéndez Pidal, R., *España, eslabón entre la Cristiandad y el Islam*, Espasa-Calpe, Madrid 1968 (2nd edn)

*Menéndez Pidal, R. (ed.), *Historia de España: (3) España Visigoda (4) España Musulmana*, 711–1031 (5) *España Musulmana, instituciones y arte*, Espasa-Calpe, Madrid 1963–5

*Menéndez Pidal, R., *Idea imperial de Carlos V* (and other essays), Espasa-Calpe, Madrid 1963 (5 th edn)

*Menéndez Pidal, R., *La España del Cid*, 2 vols, Espasa-Calpe, Madrid 1956 (5th edn)

*Michelet, J., *Histoire de la République romaine*, Flammarion, Paris 1866

Miller, T., *The Castle and the Crown*, Gollancz, London 1963

Museo Arqueológico Provincial. Catálogo de Arte Asturiano Prerrománico, Oviedo 1961

Napier, W. F. P., *History of the War in the Peninsula*, 6 vols, Thos & Wm Boone, London 1828–40

Okey, T., *Preface to Ford's "Gatherings from Spain"*, q.v.

*Pérez Galdós, B., *Gerona*, Hernando, Madrid 1948

Pérez Galdós, B., *Zaragoza*, Hernando, Madrid 1953

Petrie, Sir, C., *Philip II of Spain*, Eyre and Spottiswoode, London 1963

*Pich, J. X., *España Legendaria*, Yagües, Madrid 1934

Poema de mio Cid Saturnino Callega, Madrid 1919

Prescott, W. H., *History of the Reign of Ferdinand and Isabella the Catholic*, 2 vols, Routledge, London 1883

*Priego, J., *La Guerra de Independencia*, Gran Capitán, Madrid 1947

Purcell, M., *The Gret Captain*, Alvin Redman, London 1963

Riera Vidal, P., *The Jews of Toledo*, Toledo 1962

Roth, C., *A History of the Marranos*, Meridan Books Inc., New York 1959

*Sánchez-Albornoz, C., *La España Musulmana*, 2 vols, El Ateneo, Buenos Aires 1960 (2nd edn)

*Sánchez-Albornoz, C. & Viñas, A., *Lecturas Históricas españolas* , Taurus, Madrid 1960

Santiago Sebastián *Teruel y su provincia*, Aries, Barcelona 1959

Santillana, S. D., *Legendas españolas* , Ayax, Barcelona 1951

Scholes, P. A., *The Oxford Companion to Music*, O.U.P., London 1945 (6th edn)

Scott, Sir W., *Tales of a Grandfather*, A. & C. Black, London 1898

Sitwell, S., *Spain*, Batsford, London 1950

Sordo, E., *Moorish Spain*, Elek, London 1963

Starkie, W., *Grand Inquisitor*, Hodder & Stoughton, London 1940

Starkie, W., *The Road to Santiago*, John Murray, London 1957

Street, G. E., *Gothic Architecture in Spain*, 2 vols, Dent, London 1914

*Vicens Vives, J., *Aproximación a la historia de España*, Salvat, Barcelona 1970

Watt, W. M. & Cachia, P., *A History of Islamic Spain* (also *Spanish translation by J. Elizalde, Madrid 1970), Edinburgh University Press, Edinburgh 1965

Williams, L., *The Arts and Craft of Older Spain* 3 vols, Foulis, Edinburgh 1907

Notes

INTRODUCTION

1. Al-kantara is Arabic for "the bridge", so Puente de Alcántara means "Bridge of the bridge".
2. You may, however, be told that it was at the other side of Toledo, where the Visigothic palace is said to have stood.
3. The work of Moslems who stayed on in areas reconquered by the Christians.
4. Shaped like an inverted trough (*artesón*) and usually decorated with geometric designs and painted panels.

CHAPTER 1

1. *A History of Spain and Portugal*, p. 23
2. G. Marañón, *Las Ideas biológicas del P. Feijóo*, p. 82
3. *The Story of Civilization* (3), p. 307
4. *Decline and Fall of the Roman Empire*, ch. 27
5. Eleven of them averaged a reign of three years, twenty others averaged six and a half, and only five achieved between twelve and eighteen.
6. About A.D. 300 Arius of Alexandria launched the first great heresy of the Christian Church by declaring that the Son was *not* of the same substance as the Father.
7. Observe, and remember later on, how the Cantabrian mountains continue to nurture a "Resistance" movement.
8. C. Sánchez-Albornoz & A. Viñas, *Lecturas historicas españolas,*, p. 34
9. Witiza's sons had been promised the throne of Spain by Musa, but were content to accept estates of a thousand villages each, in settlement.

CHAPTER 2

1. *Decline and Fall of the Roman Empire*, ch. 7
2. Presumably supplanting the Church of Santa *Rufina*, still one of the patron saints of Seville.

3. *A History of Islamic Spain*, Spanish translation by J. Elizalde, p. 39
4. Correctly spelled Abd al-Rahman, "Servant of the Compassionate One", but pronounced roughly as in the text.
5. Translation by Dorothy Sayers, Penguin, London 1957
6. R. Menéndez Pidal, *Historia de España*, Madrid 1967, vol. IV p. 79 (authors translation)
7. Mohamed's tribe, to which the Omayyad and Abbassid clans belonged, a necessary condition for Caliphs, or "successors".
8. C. Sánchez-Albornoz, *La España Musulmana,* vol. 1, p. 106.

CHAPTER 3

1. C. Sánchez-Albornoz & A. Viñas, *Lecturas históricas española,* p. 63
2. I enumerate the titles because they are so often distorted and made into proper names in history books.
3. From *muluk al-tawa'if*, kings of the splinter states referred to in the text.

CHAPTER 4

1. Fourteenth century, partly by Chaucer, from the French *Roman de la Rose*, of Guillaume de Lorris and Jean de Meung.

CHAPTER 5

1. The plate on p. 102 shows the royal motto in a cartouche at either end of the lettered tile frieze. Right is a stylised version of the stepped battlements of the Mosque of Córdoba and left a good example of tile mosaic.
2. Readers will observe the mention of various currencies at the same or different times. It is impossible to translate these sums into modern units, as none had or has permanent stability. We can safely say, however, that Alfonso's eighteen year contest for an empty honour impoverished Castile.

CHAPTER 6

1. See García Mercadal, *Viajes de extranjeros por España y Portugal*, Vol. 3, p. 882
2. About ten years later the galleys of Seville ravaged the coast from Cornwall to the Thames, burning Winchelsea and Gravesend.
3. H. W. C. Davis, *Mediaeval Europe*, London 1960 (2nd edn), p. 77
4. W. Shakespeare, *King Richard III*, Act V, Sc. 4
5. According to Livermore, while Pedro was still trying to raise the money from the towns of Castile, the Black Prince was negotiating with the King of Aragon, lately Henry of Trastámara's ally, over a proposed partition of Castile.
6. His enemies alleged that his mother was a servant; historians have shown that she was the wife of the Mayor of Cañete in Aragón.

7. Bartholomé Joly, who travelled in Spain in 1603–4, gives all the details of execution by *degollando*, i.e. cutting the throat of the supine victim with a knife and then decapitating the corpse.

CHAPTER 7

1. It has been suggested that this was only because Isabel was paramount in Castile, to which Seville belonged.
2. They can be seen in the illustration on p. 33
3. *The Story of Civilization* (6), p. 209
4. Irving, *A Chronicle of the Conquest of Granada*, p. 290
5. See García Mercadal, Vol. 3, p. 1034

CHAPTER 8

1. The phrase is that of the contemporary historian, J. de Mariana.
2. This regiment was of Irish origin and its colours, still on view, display a blue harp.
3. Napier, *History of the War in the Peninsula*, Vol. 3, p. 24
4. Sir John Stuart's Anglo-Sicilian force, instead of waiting for opportunities, which never arose, of attacking Naples, could have landed at Palamos and relieved Gerona. At the same time the defenders of Gerona "failed not to remonstrate against the cold-blooded neglect of those who should have succoured them . . . and this was the moment that the Junta of Catalonia, so eloquent, so patriotic with the pen, were selling, to foreign merchants, the arms supplied by England for the defence of their country." Napier, op. cit., Vol. 3, p. 34.
5. See García Mercadal, Vol. 3, p. 1672

CHAPTER 9

1. Used in libations and sacrifices. Today's citizens call them the frying-pan and oil flask.
2. See García Mercadal, Vol. 3, p. 44
3. *History of the Dominion of the Arabs in Spain*, Vol. 1, p. 454.
4. *Gothic Architecture in Spain*, Vol. 2, p. 43.

CHAPTER 10

1. *Moorish Spain*, p. 138
2. For those who wish to study the comparison more closely Scholes' articles, including an extract from "How to play the Cinema Organ", by the aptly named Dr George Tootell, are most valuable.
3. Though its *mudéjar* work is to me the chief attraction, the inhabitants think much more of the Lovers of Teruel, to the point of calling their town "City of the Lovers". A sentimental old tale claims the same importance here as does the entirely mythical romance of Romeo and

Juliet in Verona. There, in a city teeming with the finest creations of Rome, the Middle Ages and the Renaissance, you meet only worried tourists looking for the house or the tomb of Juliet (who didn't exist), and I once saw an earnest searcher discover the house of Romeo, until a bend in the street disclosed the complete sign, reading "Alfa-Romeo". Here in Teruel there is a street called Los Amantes, another named after Hartzenbusch, who wrote a play about them, a bas-relief of them on the grand stairway below the town, a threepenny history of the lovers on sale at every bookstall and finally their statues, reclining on the caskets that enclose their alleged, mummified remains.

CHAPTER 11

1. *Don Quixote*, English translation by J. M. Cohen, Penguin Classics, London 1950, p. 54
2. These relics are responsible for the Cathedral of Oviedo, architecturally unremarkable, being known as *Sancta* in the middle ages.

CHAPTER 12

1. *Don Quixote.*
2. Ximena or Jimena was of the royal house of Asturias and a niece of Alfonso VI of León. Jimena Gómez, immortalised in ballad, play and film, has no historical existence.
3. J. Lang, *The Story of Robert the Bruce*, London n.d., p. 100; Sir W. Scott, *Tales of a Grandfather*, Black, London 1898, p. 100
4. *Spain*, p. 5
5. See García Mercadal Vol. 1, p. 265

CHAPTER 13

1. The story is not as far-fetched as it may seem; the Vargas-Carvajal family was honoured by Charles V with the privilege of displaying the imperial two-headed eagle. This is how the mighty practised economy.
2. *Gothic Architecture in Spain*, Vol. 1, p. 107

Index

Abbas Ibn Firnas, 71
Abbasids, 56, 62, 63, 75
Abderrahman I 61-66
Abderrahman III, 72, 74-79, 155
Abu Yusuf Hasday, 77
Adolphus, 47
Alcádir, 94
Alcázar, 18, 22, 32, 107, 164
Alfonso I, 186
Alfonso II, 87, 184, 185
Alfonso III, 68
Alfonso V, 190
Alfonso VI, 18-21, 28, 89-97, 165, 184
Alfonso X, 77, 98-103
Alfonso XI, 106
Alfonso XIII, 184
Alhambra Palace, 98, 164
Al-Haqem I, 65
Al-Haqem II, 77, 78, 81
Al-Khushani, 71
Almanzor, 77-83, 123, 190
Almohads, 97, 145, 159
Almoravids, 95-97, 159
Al-Mushrafí, 78-80
Alvaro de Luna, 111-114, 117
Andalucía, 46, 71, 74
Aragón, 19, 88, 105, 131
Architecture;
    Islamic, 164, 168
    Mozarabic, 29, 98, 179-184
    Plateresque, 194, 204-209
    Renaissance, 203-205, 214
    Romanesque, 191-193, 204-208
    Visigothic, 25, 82, 175
Armada, Spanish, 134, 176, 195
Asturias, 180-187
Augustina Doménech, 143-145

Barcelona, 47, 68, 128, 143
Bartholomew Casas, 137, 138
Basques, 37, 64, 74
Beltraneja, 118-120
Berbers, 15, 55-57, 61-63, 68-71, 79, 83,
    159
Berenguela, 18, 28, 32
Black Prince, 109, 110, 202
Blanche of Bourbon, 106, 107
Burgos, 195-200
Burgos, Capilla del Condestable, 195
    Cathedral, 195
    Convent de las Huelgas, 200-202

Cadiz, 99
Cantabrian Mountains, 49, 61, 85
Carthaginians, 38-40
Casanova, 151
Castile, 86, 88, 105, 109, 190
Catholic Sovereigns, 123-126
Celts, 37, 38
Celtiberians, 37, 38, 40, 41
Cervantes, 41, 56, 136, 197
Charlemagne, 64, 65, 68, 71, 185, 189
Charles II, 156
Charles III, 138, 139
Charles IV, 138, 139
Charles V, 21, 23, 107, 131-133
Cid, 21, 89-91, 96, 164, 195-200, 204,
    209
Civil War, 32, 172
Columbus, 126-130, 210
Córdoba, 62, 63, 70-81, 159-162
Córdoba Cathedral, 160-163
Cortés, 137
Covadonga, 61, 185-187
Crusades, 88

Devil's Bridge, 149, 157
De Elcano, 137
Don Quixote, 32, 132, 177, 198

El Greco, 19, 22, 23, 135, 192
Eleanor of Castile, 99
Elizabeth I, England, 134
Elizabeth of Portugal, 132
Enrique the Impotent, 105, 117-120

Fadrique, 106, 107
Ferdinand I, 89, 191
Ferdinand III, Saint, 97, 98, 190, 199
Ferdinand VII, 141, 143
Ferdinand of Aragón, 119-126
Florinda, 15, 25, 51, 60

Galib, 79-81
Galla Placidia, 47, 48, 59, 198
Gerona, 67, 139-142
Girdle of Zobeida, 27, 67, 83, 94, 96,
    112, 114, 120, 121, 132, 133, 145
Golden Age, 131-139
Goths, 47, 49, 178
Goya, 139, 141
Granada, 98, 120-123
Guadalquivir, 63, 69
Guzmán, 42, 112

Haroun al-Rashid, 67, 72
Henry of Trastámara, 105, 109-111
Hermandad, 32, 120
Hernando de Talvera, 123, 125
Hishem II, 79, 80
Hispano Romans, 43, 44, 52

Iberian, 37, 38
Ibn al Ahmar, 98
Ibn Amar, 92, 94
Ibn Hafsun, 73, 75
Inquisition, 120-124, 126, 171, 211, 212
Isabel, 117-126, 130
Islam, 55-59, 61
Islamic, 159-168

James I, Aragón, 99, 100, 105
Jews, 27, 50, 56, 72, 73, 99-102, 108, 125,
    130, 150
John of Gaunt, 108, 112, 202
John II, Castile, 112, 117
John of Görtz, 72
Juan of Aragón, 153, 154
Juana la Loca, 130
Julian, Count, 51, 57, 58

Las Navas de Toloso, 18, 19, 29
León, 60, 68, 74, 75, 77, 89, 143, 182,
    189-194

León Cathedral, 194
León, St Isidore's Church, 191-194
Lluria, Roger de, 150
Lope de Vega, 137
Luis de León, 11, 210-214

Madrid, 13, 19, 149
Málaga, 122, 123
Mansur al, 66
Maria de Monroy, 215
Maria de Padilla, 107
Mariano Alvarez, 140-142
Mary of England, 134
Mérida, 58, 59, 149
Moors, 55, 56, 70, 87, 96
Morocco, 95-97
Moslem, 52, 55, 56, 70-74, 85-89, 169
Mosque of Córdoba, 160
Mozarabs, 16, 56, 63, 68, 69, 72, 73, 98
Mudéjar, 21-23, 86, 98, 107, 165-172
Muladi, 17, 70, 73
Musa, Ibn Nusair, 51-60
Mushrafi, al, 78-80

Napoleon, 74, 139, 140, 152
Navarre, 74, 75
Numantia, 10, 40-42

Omar Ibn Hafsun, 73-75
Omayyads, 9, 15, 56, 61-69, 159
Ordónez, Garcia, 196
Ordoño the Bad, 75, 77
Oviedo, 180-185, 190
Oviedo Cathedral, 184

Palos, 128
Pamplona, 43, 64, 83
Pedro the Cruel, 105-111, 164
Peninsular War, 11, 139
Philip II, 133-135
Philip III, 135
Pilgrims, 88, 189, 190
Plateresque, 27, 194, 204-209

Reconquest, 85-90, 96, 97, 105, 189
Renaissance, 203-205, 214
Roderick, 15, 25, 51, 60
Roland, Prince, 64
Roland, Bishop of Arles, 70
Romans, 17, 37-47, 149-151, 178
Romanesque, 191-193, 204, 208
Roman remains, 14, 19, 23, 149-151
Ruby of Granada, 107, 110

Salamanca, 204-215, 221
Salamanca Cathedral, 206-208
Salamanca, Casa de la Conches, 205
Sancho the Fat, 75, 77

Sancho Panza, 9, 27, 32
Santiago, 97, 189
Santiago, St James, 81, 87, 88, 202
Segovia, 149, 150
Seville, 58, 60, 69, 92, 100, 169
Seville, Alcázar, 107, 164
Seville Cathedral, 108, 130
Siege of Gerona, 139-142
Siege of Zaragoza, 143
Soria, 41
St Casilda, 15, 19, 90
St Bartholomew, 156
St Isidore, 15, 50, 89, 91, 96, 177-179,
    191
St James, see Santiago
St Narcissus, 140
St Vincent, 169

Table of Solomon, 58-60
Tagus, 14, 19, 25
Tarif, 51, 56, 57
Tarik, 50, 57-60
Tarragona, 149-157
Teruel, 170-172
Theodosius, 45, 46

Toledo, 13-16, 18-34, 50, 69, 73, 74, 94,
    96, 102, 103
Toledo, Alcázar, 22, 32
Toledo Cathedral, 28, 29
Tortosa, 143, 145
Trastámaras, 105-116

Valencia, 94, 105, 143
Visigoths, 15, 19, 29, 47-53, 57-59, 60,
    61, 85
Visigothic style, 25, 82, 89, 175, 176
    60, 61

Wellington, 9, 139, 143, 214
Witiza, 50, 51, 187

Ysabel, 119
Yusuf Ibn Tasufin, 95, 96

Zobeida, 67
Zobeida, girdle of, 27, 67, 83, 94, 96, 112,
    114, 120, 132, 145
Zaragoza, 41, 64, 69, 143
Zaragoza, siege of, 143
Ziryab, 72
Zorrilla, 26